THE GOSPEL OF OUT OF DOORS

Francis E. Clark

President of the World's Christian Endeavor Union

Author of "Old Homes of New Americans," "The Continent of Opportunity," "In the Footsteps of St. Paul," "The Holy Land of Asia Minor," "Our Italian Fellow Citizens," etc.

First Fruits Press
Wilmore, Kentucky
c2015

The gospel of out of doors, by Francis E. Clark.

First Fruits Press, ©2015
Previously published: New York : Association Press, ©1920.

ISBN: 9781621714217 (print), 9781621714224 (digital)

Digital version at http://place.asburyseminary.edu/christianendeavorbooks/9/

Clark, Francis E. (Francis Edward), 1851-1927.
    The gospel of out of doors/ Francis E. Clark.
    viii, 143 pages ; 21 cm.
    Wilmore, Ky. : First Fruits Press, ©2015.
    Reprinted from various periodicals.
    Reprint. Previously published: New York : Association Press, ©1920.
    ISBN: 9781621714217 (pbk.)
    1. Natural history -- Outdoor books. I. Title.
QH81 .C5 2015

Cover design by Jonathan Ramsay

asburyseminary.edu
800.2ASBURY
204 North Lexington Avenue
Wilmore, Kentucky 40390

First Fruits
THE ACADEMIC OPEN PRESS OF ASBURY SEMINARY

First Fruits Press

The Academic Open Press of Asbury Theological Seminary

204 N. Lexington Ave., Wilmore, KY 40390

859-858-2236

first.fruits@asburyseminary.edu

asbury.to/firstfruits

THE GOSPEL
OF OUT OF DOORS

FRANCIS E. CLARK

President of the World's Christian Endeavor Union

*Author of "Old Homes of New Americans," "The
Continent of Opportunity," "In the Footsteps of
St. Paul," "The Holy Land of Asia Minor,"
"Our Italian Fellow Citizens," etc.*

ASSOCIATION PRESS

New York: 347 Madison Avenue
1920

Acknowledgments are due, for permission to republish these chapters, to *The Christian Endeavor World, The Outlook, The Continent, The Christian Herald, and Suburban Life.*

To my grandchildren,

> ALDEN HASKELL CLARK,
>
> RUTH EMERSON CHASE,
>
> FRANCIS CLARK CHASE,
>
> FRANCIS EDWARD CLARK, 2nd,
>
> MARGERY JACQUELINE CLARK,
>
> ELEANOR WILLISTON CHASE,

for whom the Old Farm already holds so many out-of-door joys. May these joys increase as they and the farm grow older together.

CONTENTS

WHY THIS BOOK WAS WRITTEN

There are two kinds of books. One kind couldn't be helped. The other kind could be helped, but their writers were compelled to write, by a sense of duty to a cause or an idea, or they were written with an eye to the royalties. Not that one kind is necessarily any better than the other. The author of the couldn't-be-helped book may maunder on about his favorite subject as a lover babbles about his mistress, never quite happy unless he can find a sympathetic ear into which he can pour her charms. The author of the could-be-helped book may bring to his tasks the research of a student and the industry of a lifetime, and produce a work that the world will not willingly let die. But I venture to say that the author of the couldn't-be-helped book will enjoy himself more while he is at work on it, and will not quarrel with the world if his book doesn't prove to be a "best seller."

I will confess without a blush that this book is of the latter class. I have come under the spell of the out of doors on the old farm. It would be hard not to write about it even if nobody read what I wrote. Like an old minister whom I once knew, who, after he retired from active service, though he never expected to preach again, still wrote a sermon for his barrel every week, so I should be inclined, if worst came to worst, to write about my farm, even if my essays were to be forever confined to the unsympathetic embrace of a drawer in my study desk. However, a number of partial friends have expressed their pleasure in some of these essays, when published in various periodicals, and it requires but a slight amount of such encouragement to incline one to bind the children of his love between boards and give them to the world. I have, too, a purpose not altogether egoistic in their publication, and that is that other men and women, encouraged by my own experience of the joy, the comfort, and the health that come from an old farm, may feel its lure, learn its joy, and experience its health-giving comforts.

F. E. C.

CHAPTER I

THE GOSPEL OF OUT OF DOORS

"Gospel," in its derivation as well as in its modern meaning, simply means *good news*. This book was written to preach the Gospel of Out of Doors. If we really understand this gospel, every tree and shrub, every flower and fern, every star in the heavens and every fleecy cloud that veils them, will say to us, as Mt. Blanc shouted in the ears of Coleridge, "God, *God*, GOD."

This Gospel of Out of Doors is the most efficacious antidote for the peculiar evils of our own day and generation. These are the evils of the city, not of the country. The reeking misery of the slums, not the stolid animalism of the fields, is our danger in America today. Anarchy is hatched in the city. The brothel is a product of the city. The "gang" has no room for its operations except in the city. Bribery and political corruption, "graft" of every sort, find their hotbed in the city. If by some master stroke the slums could be transported to the Vermont hills or the Adirondack woods or the South

Dakota prairies, as Adam was put in the Garden of Eden to dress it and to keep it, half the problems of our everyday civilization would be solved.

If, at the same time with this removal of the submerged tenth, the equally submerged members of the Four Hundred at the other end of the social scale—the men and women submerged in the petty requirements of society, submerged in selfishness, in greed, and in indifference to their country, their political duties, and their fellowmen, submerged in depths of moral iniquity that so often culminates in the divorce court—if these men could also be planted in another garden and made to dress it and keep it, pretty nearly the other half of our national problems would be solved, "for then justice will spring out of the ground, and righteousness will look down from Heaven."

No nation was ever overthrown by its farmers. Chaldea and Egypt, Greece and Rome, grew rotten and ripe for destruction not in the fields, but in the narrow lanes and crowded city streets and in the palaces of their nobility. So let us thank God and take courage as we see in our day any movement, however halting, countryward; the "abandoned farm" no longer abandoned; the long

[2]

and ceaseless line of hardy immigrants moving northwestward to take up the yet unfurrowed fields; the country homes made possible by the bicycle and the automobile; the increasing interest in wholesome athletic sports; the fascination of nature study for our boys and girls; and the "call of the wild," heard in these days from so many quarters and in such eager, imperative tones.

Surely the history of the creation repeats itself in every generation, and constantly is the Lord God taking man and putting him in a new garden "to dress it and to keep it." As the Psalmist called upon the dragons and all deeps, fire and hail, snow and vapor, stormy wind fulfilling His word, to praise the Lord from the earth, why may we not reverently call upon bicycle and automobile, steam train and trolley car fulfilling His word, to praise Him also, for these are His modern instruments for taking men out of the city streets and scattering them upon the face of the earth.

Just as the slums were becoming more slummy, reeking more and more with the moral filth of the gutter; just as the commercial spirit seemed to be prostrating itself absolutely before the dollar sign, saying, "We will have no gods before thee"; just as

[3]

our complex, artificial life seemed to be lording it completely over the slower, simpler life of our fathers—in a single quarter century God called these new modes of locomotion into being and opened fresh fields and pastures new to jaded humanity, and at the same time created in our nation a hunger for the soil and a love for outdoors such as it had not known before.

Why should not any lover of his kind call a motorcycle "a means of grace," if its invention reveals God's glories in nature to a million city-begrimed toilers? The favored few cross continents or oceans to see a famous picture or a lovely landscape, but here is a little affair with two wheels and some steering-gear that can show its owner a thousand beautiful nature pictures every year, and, while he is journeying to them, give him, at the same time, health and muscle and length of days.

Whatever may be said against the athletics of the day—and a strong case can be made out against the brutality of some, the gambling spirit that goes with others, and the undue absorption of the American people in the sporting pages of the daily paper—this thought mitigates, if it does not cover, a multitude of their sins, that they are the practical preachers of the Gospel of Out of Doors to a multitude who otherwise would know little about it. Few of these sports can be indulged in under cover; none but the most degrading and degraded are indigenous to city life. The acknowledged moral superiority of American students to those in many continental universities, which every traveler must admit, is due in no small part, I believe, to the rigorous training of the college navy and the football field, and the high physical standard demanded of the trained athlete. Over-indulgence, impurity, licentiousness, received a staggering blow among educated American men when the diamond was marked off, the running track laid out, and football goals were erected.

But my subject is not one of abstract theory, it is not limited to the farmer or the athlete or to any particular class of favored mortals, for God's air and sunlight are free to all. God's pictures are painted on nature's ever-varying canvas for everyone. It is only a matter of our looking. To every one who has legs to walk or a wheel to ride, and eyes to see, they are all free, for God never shuts up His best gifts in a gallery or makes them dependent on the size of a bank account.

What, then, may the Gospel of Out of

[5]

Doors do for each one of us? It may bring us back to the simple life which this feverish, artificial age so sadly lacks. "The least crumb of reality," says Charles Wagner, "an ant at work, a child at play, a leaf falling to the ground, has always strangely fascinated me. A part of the great human drama is played there, without paint or attitudinizing. The attraction of living things is inexhaustible. Each one of them by an irresistible movement becomes a sign, lesson, symbol. There is no rivulet, however small, that does not conduct to the sea. There is not a hidden pathway in the valley which, step by step, does not lead up to the height. The whole creation talks to him who knows how to lend an ear."

Especially is this out-of-doors outlook and uplook needed by the so-called educated man, whose learning smells altogether of the library or the laboratory. There is an intellectual exclusiveness which is only one shade less offensive to God and man alike than the snobbery of wealth, an educated Philistinism that is as ruthless in its prejudices and as narrow in its outlook on life as the view of a Patagonian. Books, books, and what can be dug out of books, or put into books, is all of life to some. Such need to learn that

"One impulse from the vernal wood
   May teach you more of man,
Of moral evil and of good,
   Than all the sages can."

Then there is a blessed freedom that comes only to the man out of doors, a liberty of spirit, an unswathing of the bands of convention and custom, an expansion of soul which is learned by those who know God in nature.

"Seas roll to waft me,
   Suns to light me rise,
My footstool Earth,
   My canopy the skies,"

sings Pope, or, as Wordsworth phrases it,

"I care not, Fortune, what you may deny,
   You cannot rob me of free nature's grace;
You cannot shut the windows of the sky,
   Through which Aurora shows her brightening face."

But if we would quote poetry, let us turn to the poetry of the Book of books, for the Gospel of Out of Doors is often interpreted by the Bible, and in turn largely helps us to understand the Bible. When the Psalmist would declare the greatness of Jehovah, he takes us

[7]

out of doors with him, and bids us look up at
the stars, and mark the fleet-winged chariot
of the cloud, and listen to the voice of the
wind.

"O Jehovah my God, thou art very great;
  Thou art clothed with honor and majesty;
  Who coverest thyself with light as with a
      garment;
  Who stretchest out the heavens like a cur-
      tain;
  Who layeth the beams of his chambers in
      the waters;
  Who maketh the clouds his chariot;
  Who walketh upon the wings of the wind."

Then the thought of the singer turns
from the mighty and terrible to the quiet
and gentle out-of-door scenes, which tell him
just as much of God: the gurgling, gurgling
brook trickling down the hillside, the peaceful cattle drinking at the stream, the birds
singing in the trees.

"He sendeth forth springs into the valleys;
  They run among the mountains;
  They give drink to every beast of the field;
  The wild asses quench their thirst,
  By them the fowl of the heaven have their
      habitation;

[8]

They sing among the branches. . . .
He causeth the grass to grow for the cattle,
And herb for the service of man."

But the winds and the thunder-cloud, and the quiet pastoral scenes, do not exhaust God's goodness; "the sea is His, and He made it."

"Yonder is the sea, great and wide,
Wherein are things creeping innumerable,
Both small and great beasts.
There go the ships;
There is leviathan whom thou hast formed
    to play therein.
These all wait for thee,
That thou mayest give them their food in
    due season."

Was anything more exquisite ever penned than the Psalmist's description of springtime and summer?

"Thou visitest the earth, and waterest it,
Thou greatly enrichest it; the river of God
    is full of water. . . .
Thou makest it soft with showers; thou
    blessest the springing thereof.
Thou crownest the year with thy goodness;
And thy paths drop fatness.

[9]

They drop upon the pastures of the wilder-
    ness:
And the hills are girded with joy.
The pastures are clothed with flocks;
The valleys are also covered over with
    corn;
They shout for joy, they also sing."

We turn to that wonderful poem called
the Book of Job, the book which Froude declared, when it was fully understood, would
be seen towering up alone, above all the
poetry of the world, and we hear Jehovah
Himself rebuking the one-sided arguments
of Eliphaz and the youthful presumptuous-
ness of Elihu, as well as the despairing pes-
simism of Job's wail of anguish, by taking
them all, as it were, out of doors, and show-
ing them His invincible might in the heavens
above, and the earth beneath, and the waters
under the earth—a sight which calmed their
nervousness and rebuked their littleness, and
led Job to cry out in lowly reverence: "I
have heard of Thee with the hearing of the
ear, but now mine eye seeth Thee, where-
fore I abhor myself and repent in dust and
ashes."

And this is the way God brought the pa-
triarch to Himself; not by argument, not by

[10]

philosophy, but by declaring His might and beauty in the invisible world:

"Where wast thou when I laid the founda-
    tions of the earth?
Declare, if thou hast understanding.
Who determined the measures thereof, if
    thou knowest?
Or who stretched the line upon it?
Whereupon were the foundations thereof
    fastened?
Or who laid the corner stone thereof;
When the morning stars sang together,
And all the sons of God shouted for
    joy? . . .
Canst thou bind the cluster of the Pleiades,
Or loose the bands of Orion?
Canst thou lead forth the signs of the Zo-
    diac[1] in their season?
Or canst thou guide the Bear with her
    train?"

When Isaiah, stern prophet of retribution as he is, tells of God's goodness to a repent-ant people, he must go out of doors to find his smiles. It is in the mountains and the hills, in the fir trees and the myrtles, that he finds the symbol of God's everlasting loving-kindness.

---

[1] Margin.

[11]

"For the mountains may depart,
And the hills be removed;
But my lovingkindness shall not depart
     from thee,
Neither shall my covenant of peace be re-
     moved."

"For ye shall go out with joy,
And be led forth with peace:
The mountains and the hills shall break
     forth before you into singing,
And all the trees of the field shall clap their
     hands.
Instead of the thorn shall come up the fir
     tree;
And instead of the brier shall come up the
     myrtle tree:
And it shall be to Jehovah for a name,
For an everlasting sign that shall not be cut
     off."

But not only David and Job and Isaiah,
but He who spake as never man spake, takes
us into the open with Him. His greatest sermon was preached from the pulpit of a rough
hillside while His audience sat upon the
grass. He stood in the stern of a little boat,
tossing upon the gentle waves, while His
hearers lined the shore. He told them of the
lilies, one of which He could perhaps pluck
as He spoke, and hold before them. He

[12]

talked of the birds, which perhaps sang to the people while He talked about them. The mustard seed is not too small, and the mountain which might be removed and cast into the sea is not too large, to illustrate His lesson of faith. He went fishing with His disciples, and spent His nights of prayer not in an oratory, but on the mountain side.

Then, as we close, let us come back, led by our Lord's gentle hand, to our thought at the beginning that the good tidings of outdoors, like every other gospel, is to bring us to God the Father in this great world—our Father's house.

Nature hath many voices, but one theme. Many instruments are in her orchestra, but they are all tuned to the same key. They all tell of His infinite might and majesty and power. Let us then, as we walk abroad, think of hills and valleys, not alone as agricultural possibilities; of leaf and tree not only from the forester's standpoint; of purling brook in summer or icy lake in winter not simply as places for sport, but of each as a messenger to lead our spirit upward and onward.

"Oh what a glory doth the world put on,
  For him who with a fervent heart goes forth

[13]

Under the bright and glorious sky, and
  looks
On duties well performed and days well
  spent!
For him the wind, ay, and the yellow leaves,
Shall have a voice, and give him eloquent
  teachings."

Indeed, these eloquent teachings will not
narrow or dwarf our souls by telling us of
anything sordid and mean and selfish, but
they will speak of duty and privilege, of love
and hope, of right and wrong, of man and
God, and with Browning we can cry:

"I trust in nature for the stable laws
  Of beauty and utility. Spring shall plant,
  And Autumn garner to the end of time:
  I trust in God—the right shall be the right,
  And other than the wrong while he en-
    dures:
  I trust in my own soul, that can perceive
  The outward and the inward, nature's
    good and God's."

CHAPTER II

THE JOY OF THE SEED CATALOGUE

They began to come a month ago, these delicious bits of good literature—sweet harbingers of spring. As I write, the blizzard of the winter is howling around my north windows; the snow lies a foot deep on the piazza and the lawn—even the hardy blue jay no longer scolds his mate from the big pine tree at the back door, but is trying to find scant shelter from the Arctic winds in the thicker woods. Yet even my sympathy for him and other two-legged tramps cannot altogether dull my joy, for a bright fire is blazing upon the hearth—and the seed catalogues have come. I have been saving them up for a month for just such a cozy, indoor afternoon as this, that I might gloat over them, and conjure up pictures of greenery and bloom which, without them, would seem so far away.

Shall I begin at the vegetable or the flower end of my catalogues? I think with the former, for they deserve the place of honor by the good old rule that "handsome is as

[15]

handsome does." I will begin, too, at the very beginning. I will not even skip the title page or the preface, lest I might miss that new squash that is put upon the market for the first time this year.

"O squash rich and mellow, with insides of yellow," as the seed catalogue poet rhapsodizes, "just list while I sing a few lines; product that's greater, from beet to potater, ne'er grew on a husbandman's vines! A Hubbard squash dinner is always a winner, a solace, a balm and a boon; it cheers and refreshes, and breaks up the meshes of sorrow at noon. Who was it invented the large, pleasant-scented and life-saving squash we adore? Let's crown him with laurel and bay leaves and sorrel, and honor his name evermore!"

But the poet's eulogy of the squash shall not cause me to forget the humble snap bean and the prosaic beet, and I read with absolute conviction that the "mammoth bean pods are eight or ten inches long, as thick as our finger, very fleshy and thick meated, while the color is a rich golden yellow, very clear and waxlike." I further read that the beets are "smooth and round, exceedingly sweet and tender, and never coarse, tough, or stringy." To be sure, I am a trifle staggered by reflecting that there are ten kinds of beans and eight kinds of beets, each of which is, apparently, a little better than all the others. But I reflect that these vegetables are undoubtedly like the headgear the rival hatters presented to President Lincoln, and of which he said, "Gentlemen, your hats mutually surpass each other." I have no doubt that if I had all the ten kinds of beans and the eight kinds of beets on the table before me, I would use as many superlatives as the seed catalogue man himself. How can one write sedately, or remember "the power of an undue statement," when he is writing on such subjects as fresh beets and string beans?

I read on and rejoice in the prospects of "cucumbers of enormous size, great beauty, perfect shape, and rich dark green color, the flesh compact, fine-grained, sparkling white, and of a most refreshing and delightful flavor," of lettuce that "almost melts in the mouth, crisp, tender, sweet, and white," of a potato that is "particularly mild and delicious," and of a tomato of which it is said, "when once grown, all others are discarded." Now come the pages devoted to corn. Can you not see the tall, stately stalks with the ears, "three on every stalk," peeping out from be-

[17]

neath the broadswords of leaves? And as your imagination runs riot in the cornfield of next August you feel that the seed catalogue man has scarcely done justice to the subject when he writes of the "deep, succulent kernels, of a rich, translucent, cream-yellow color, tender, deliciously melting, and sweet." And the melons, both musk and water—what dictionary contains adjectives enough to describe them fairly and fully? The catalogue man has evidently fallen down woefully, when he can only speak of a muskmelon as "spicy in flavor, the meat thick, fine-grained, and very rich," or of a watermelon, "no matter what we say, its delicious quality and sugary sweetness will astonish you when you eat it." That last sentence shows how tired he is, how adjectives pall, and descriptions utterly fail to describe. So I will turn to the flower end of the catalogue, on the principle that the boy saves the sweetest cooky for the end of the meal.

Just look at them, these wonderful morning glories of a thousand shades, covering the whole side of a house, and sweet peas as big as dahlias, and twice as fragrant. They even seem to give their delicate odor to the printer's ink which pictures them. And the monster carnations! Let your imagination

[18]

run riot on the golden carnation, "with its exquisite fragrance, petals deeply serrated, and color dark yellow, with a few faint marks of pink"! See the soldier-like hollyhocks standing up stiffly beside the old farmhouse in their many-colored uniforms, and the peony bed arrayed in such colors as Queen Cleopatra or Joseph in his variegated coat never aspired to! View in imagination, stimulated by the seed catalogue, the modest, brown-coated mignonette, making no bid for popularity, except to the nostrils, but its remembrance lingering there, when its more gaudy companions are forgotten. Think of the roses rambling over the porch, or climbing over the garden wall, and filling the whole landscape with their exquisite beauty, and the wistaria dropping its long and lovely fronds, while it says to you, "Can you find anything more perfect and graceful than my purple clusters?"

I glance out of the window again after an hour with my seed catalogues. Can it be that it is still snowing, that the ground is still white, and all the trees bare, except where a few brown birch leaves still cling to the young trees, until the spring buds shall push them off? Well, perhaps it is winter, yet I have but to turn from the window and take up my catalogues again, to see the vegetables in my garden waiting to be picked, and the roses climbing over the wall, and the hollyhocks standing in soldierly rows behind the house, and the sweet peas breathing out their fragrance over all. Thanks for your catalogues, O seedmen; I will sit down this very afternoon and send you my first order for the new year of fruits and flowers.

CHAPTER III

THE LURE OF THE OLD FARM

"Christianity is not like butter," said a Christian Chinese to his Confucian neighbors who had come to hear about his new religion, "you don't have to learn to like it." So is the love of the land with most normal people. Tobacco is an acquired habit—you have to learn to like it, as a Chinese has to learn to like butter. Raw oysters and olives usually have to be practiced upon by most people before they can swallow them without a grimace, but land hunger is as universal as the liking for strawberries and cream. To be sure, there is here and there an abnormal person who is poisoned by strawberries, and whose stomach rebels at cream, but they are what a politician, when talking of the third or fourth party, calls a "negligible quantity."

Love of the land is substantially universal. Revolutions have been fanned into flame by land hunger, continents have been peopled by the same appetite. "Pike's Peak or Bust," was the motto of the land-hungry pilots of the prairie schooner in the forties and fifties.

[21]

The Bolsheviki of Russia acquired their great following by appealing to this universal instinct, and even the rock-ribbed Tories of England see the handwriting on the wall, and know that some time their great estates must be divided, or at least reduced in size, to give "honest John Tompkins, the hedger and ditcher" a piece of the earth that he may call his own. The writer of the famous couplet, who told us that honest John, "though he always was poor, never wished to be richer," was fooling himself and the people for whom and to whom he wrote. Honest John across the seas, though he may not have sighed for the wealth of the Indies, always did and always will want a piece of old England. Then why thwart a primeval instinct, when most of you who read this book can gratify it by a little self-sacrifice and forethought?

To be sure, the lure of the farm is not always felt in early life, especially if one is born on a farm. To be strictly honest, I must admit that many boys are lured away from the farm by their early experiences. The glare of the city streets dazzles their eyes, the movie shows and the bustle and excitement of town life make the old farm seem tame and lonesome, and many a good farmer has thus been spoiled to make a fourth-class counter-jumper. But Nature has her revenges, as well as her compensations, and this same boy, when twenty or thirty years have added discretion to his enterprise, and cooled his impatient blood, is likely to sigh, "Oh, that I had a piece of solid land and an old farmhouse that I could call my own, instead of a sixth-floor back apartment, and a view of the chimney-pot of my next neighbors!"

No, the lure of the farm is not likely to be an experience of hot-blooded youth. We are told that the cripple at the Beautiful Gate of the temple whom Peter healed was in middle life. In the words of Scripture, "The man was more than forty years old on whom this miracle of healing was wrought." I think that is about the age on which this other miracle of healing is usually wrought, and that then the farm begins to call one back to generous Mother Earth from which he sprang. Then most men begin to be healed of the blindness which in early life prevented them from seeing the beauty of the opening bud, the delicacy of the first catkin, and the peculiar lusciousness of the first peach from one's own orchard. Then one begins to learn that the most delicious "Delicious" apple from the Yakima Valley cannot compare in flavor with the old-fashioned Baldwin from the tree which he himself has planted, tended, trimmed, sprayed, and guarded from the ravages of gypsy moth and codling moth and scale and borer. Then he finds that the lowly violet on his own farm, or the lady's-slipper which springs uncared for among his own pine needles, is dearer to him than a whole shopful of floral beauties.

There is no doubt about it—Mother Earth calls her children with many voices. The frogs and froglets in the early spring when the ice goes out of the ponds, the wild geese winging their way north, the bluebirds and robins in their love-making, the rustle of the new-born leaves on the poplar trees, the bay of the hound, the whinny of the horse scenting the oats, the lowing of the mother cow anxious about her absent calf—yes, even the satisfied grunt of the pig at the trough—are calls to the old farm that are hard to resist. There are still subtler lures than these that Mother Earth uses in calling her children back to her bosom. The scent of the soil newly turned by the plowshare, the sight of the first spear of corn peering above the brown soil, the howling of a spring gale around the northeast windows, the crackling

[24]

of the birch logs in the big fireplace—these are all sights and sounds which you can find to perfection nowhere else except upon the old farm.

From forty to fifty or sixty the lure of the farm grows stronger with each passing year, but I would not advise the man on whom the miracle of healing begins to be wrought to put off all action much beyond his fourth decade—the uncertainties of life are too grave, and he may lose altogether, not only the joy of the farm, but the joy of farm-hunting, if he feels himself too rich in time and squanders his patrimony of days and months. Yet let not the man who is beginning to get his eyes open and who sees trees as men walking, go at his quest too rashly or hurriedly. He will lose part of the pleasure that should be coming to him, if he does not spend two or three years in farm-hunting. Isaak Walton tells us that we should treat the worm upon our hook as though we loved it; so the business of farm-hunting should be gone about deliberately and lovingly, lest we find at last that we have caught the wrong fish.

To be sure, the man with ancestral acres or the one who knows of an old family homestead, which he is bound to buy back, is deprived of the pleasure of farm-hunting, for there is only one farm for him, however near the North Pole or the Everglades of Florida it may lie. But most of us can enjoy the delights of farm-hunting until the place is discovered that comes the nearest possible to fitting our tastes and our pocketbooks. We will first consult the advertising columns of some farm agency. What a bewildering lot of "snaps" there are—fertile acres, fruitful orchards, a wood lot from which in imagination we have already cut the logs that glow and sparkle in our big fireplace of a winter's evening, "a cosy little five acres just right for a hen farm," another one bordering a fresh-water pond full of fish. Who could not be satisfied, especially when the prices range from $500 to $50,000? Every taste and every purse surely can be fitted to a T.

My own requirements were a little farm but a diversified one, of upland and valley, within sight of the sea, and within hearing of the roaring of the waves, plenty of old apple trees in whose hollow trunks the yellow-hammers might make their nests—I would not let a tree surgeon plaster them up for any money—some land where I might plant a young orchard according to my taste, a sufficient amount of woodland to keep the

[26]

home fires burning, not too much arable land—not more than enough for one hired man to cultivate—a chance of course to keep a cow, a pig, and some hens, to say nothing of dogs and cats, and an old house with plenty of fireplaces, and preferably with a ghost. Together with a good lady whose farm-hunger, though it sometimes had to be stimulated, measurably kept up with my own, I sought the ideal farm. We had no end of fun reading the advertisements and allowing our fancies to paint them in still more glowing colors, though that was unnecessary, and occasionally we took an excursion into the country to look at a promising prospect, only to have our hopes shattered, though we got more than enough fun out of it to pay for our carfares and our time.

Some ten years we hunted for our ideal—*our* ideal, not yours, my reader, for it would be as unfortunate if we all wanted the same farm, as if all men wanted to wed the same woman—and at last we found it. Yes, we found exactly the one that had been abandoned for us. It was within sight and sound of the sea. It was small but marvelously diversified for its few acres. It had plenty of old apple-trees and a chance for young ones. It had wood enough to last, with ju-

[27]

dicious cutting, for fifty years. It had room enough for a small menagerie of animals. It had a farmhouse more than two hundred years old and incredibly dilapidated, but with five fireplaces, and possibilities of repair—yes, and it had a ghost. It was such an utterly abandoned old farm that no one in the vicinity wanted to try to reform it, but this was an advantage, for it came within the compass of my lean pocket-book.

Now, Brother Man, go thou and do likewise. Begin your hunt when you are forty, if you have not yet reached the end of life's first semester. If you have, lose no time, and before you are fifty you, too, believe me, will find your ideal, unless you are intolerably "difficult," as the New England housewife would call you. Remember this, too, Brother Man—the time is coming when you should not let your business drive you

> "Like a galley slave at night
> Scourged to his dungeon,"

when your people will want a younger minister, your clients a younger lawyer. Then, if you have yielded to the lure of the farm, have diligently and successfully hunted and captured the right one, you will have something to interest you all the rest of your days. You will not die before your time, of inanition or ennui, as so many men have done when advancing years compel them to drop their old interests, but your last days will be your best days, and you will be gathered to your fathers like one of your own shocks of corn, fully ripe.

CHAPTER IV

A SERMON TO MY BROTHER
WEEDS

If I had been St. Francis, I would certainly have addressed a sermon to the weeds. It was all very well for him to preach to the birds, especially since all the pictures show how attentive were his feathered brethren. Nor do I wonder that St. Anthony exhorted his brother fishes, because the people of Rimini would not listen to him. It must be so, for they have commemorated the fact by building a chapel, which I have seen, on the banks of a canal near the Rubicon, to the preacher and his "Brother Fish." There have been many fishermen preachers, but only one preacher to fish, and he surely deserves his piscine chapel. Many preachers doubtless have wished that they had even fish to turn to, from an unresponsive audience. But in none of their voluminous biographies have I read that either of these saints preached to the weeds, as I am often tempted to, since I feel that my kinship with them is so close.

[30]

If a preacher can exhort effectively only those whose tendencies and temptations he has himself known, most of us are particularly well qualified to address our brother weeds. It is a wise homiletical rule to preach *ad hominem,* and to let your auditors know that you sympathize with them and understand their peculiarities.

My sermon to weeds would be something as follows:

Beloved brethren, we, your fellow-mortals, have much in common with you. In the morning we flourish and grow up; in the evening we are cut down and wither. Our brief day is but a little longer than yours. Indeed, it may be shorter; for some of you, I note, are perennials, and very loath to die, while our days are numbered from the beginning. I notice, too, that most of you are very persistently bent on taking the wrong course, and in this respect, too, we acknowledge our kinship.

Brother Burdock, you have long and exceedingly tough roots. I sometimes think they are clinched on the other side of the globe. You are much inclined to spring up in our lawns where you are not wanted. Alas! our own evil propensities are just as deep-rooted; and when we think we have

[31]

cut off the evil thing, and believe that it will trouble us no more, we soon find that we have but clipped the top of our passions, and that their roots stretch down into the depths of our being.

Brother Pursley, you, too, have the same faults, and I find you among my peas and in my strawberry bed, where your room is far better than your company. But how can we reproach you for persistently crowding out your betters when we find that with our own best thoughts and actions evil is mixed! Into our prayers even sometimes wandering thoughts intrude. I fear that some of us gave an extra five dollars to the hospital because, though it was more than we could afford, our name had to appear on a sub-scription paper next to that of a richer neighbor, and we could not drop our offering into the anonymous seclusion of a contribu-tion-box.

And you, too, Brother Poison Ivy, even with you we must claim kinship, however unwillingly. Like many a bad habit, you are quite bewitchingly beautiful in your early days. In the spring you put forth your three finely veined and tinted leaves, and twine lovingly about any support you may find. If you find none, you stand upright and inde-

pendent. But how you do multiply yourself, sending out far-reaching roots, stretch-
ing in every direction, until the ground is a
perfect network of your fibers! You
strangle every delicate thing to which you
attach yourself, and poison some people
who do but breathe the same atmosphere.

Many of us know your prototype too well.
Those little bad habits, begun when we were
boys—what a lot of trouble they gave us
before they were rooted out! We are not
sure that their virus is dead yet. The harmless, pretty little thing at the beginning—
mere good fellowship, harmless conviviality,
it seemed, but it strangled a life and poisoned
a whole family when it was grown. Moreover, you sow your evil seeds at the same
time that you stretch your runners underground, until you have a million children
and many square rods of my farm are covered with your noxious growth. I cannot
deny it. The sins of us mortals multiply in
very much the same way. One leads to another and another and another, until the
good soil of human nature that was meant
to grow virtues and good deeds is often pre-
occupied with a rank and poisonous moral
vegetation.

Brother Witch Grass, I must not forget

[33]

to reprobate you. How innocent you look when your first green shoot appears above the brown soil of springtime! You would deceive the very elect, for you look exactly like your succulent brother, Herd's Grass, but, if we let you grow, your tangle of roots and worthless shoots will choke every decent plant in the neighborhood.

There are others of your tribe which give me a lot of trouble, and yet I do not like to class them with Brother Poison Ivy and Brother Burdock and Brother Witch Grass. I refer to you, Brothers Daisy and Buttercup and Dandelion. You are very pretty and not without your uses, I admit. You brighten a field, and are quite as exquisite in your way as many of the flowers we cultivate and cherish. But you have the vice of overdoing your virtues and obtruding them where they are not wanted.

You, Brother Daisy, get into the mowing-grass, and then you become a Whiteweed, and we farmers have little patience with you. You, Brother Buttercup, do the same thing, and spoil next winter's fodder; and as for you, Brother Dandelion, you are the pest of our lawns. Yet we cannot reproach you too severely, when we remember how our own virtues tend to vices. We think they are "daisies," and so they are; but they sometimes get so rampant as to choke out other and more important virtues. They lead us to the sins to which we have no mind. Often they get into our neighbor's fields, and they hide all his special merits, so that we cannot see them ourselves, while we become a nuisance to him and he wishes we were farther away. Neatness is most admirable, yet a good wife's fear of a speck of dirt on the kitchen floor often makes the men-folks uncomfortable. Self-sacrifice is one of man's noblest virtues; but when it develops into a self-imposed, lifelong martyrdom, it is worse than buttercups in the mowing patch. Executive ability is indispensable in its place; but when it undertakes to regulate every one's actions, it is as much out of place as a crop of dandelions on the front lawn.

There are other brothers, which I think must be classed as weeds, though they can be used in times of famine. Brother Sorrel, Brother Wild Cherry, and Brother Milkweed, I refer to you. Brothers Sorrel and Milkweed make a possible salad when we are reduced to extremities, but how much better it would be if the ground you occupy were filled by Brothers Chard and Lettuce. Brother Oxheart Cherry takes no more room

[35]

in my orchard than Brother Chokecherry, but how delicious is the one and how puckery the other!

Yet I must not blame you until I clear my own moral garden of the third best and fourth best, when I might have first best, virtues growing there. I am not often more than five minutes late to church, but I might just as well be on time. I conscientiously give a tenth of my income in charity, but I am sure that with a little extra self-denial I could give a fifth. I never intend to retail any choice morsel of scandal about my neighbors, but I sometimes listen while others roll it under their tongues. Henceforth I will strive to plant whole virtues instead of half virtues in the garden of my soul.

Finally and lastly, this leads me to say, Brother Weeds, I know of but one way to keep you where you belong, and that is to fill your places with a useful growth. I have noticed that peas and pursley, like everything else, obey the law of the impenetrability of matter. They cannot occupy the same spot at the same time. I can cultivate beans or burdocks, but not both in the same garden-patch; for you, Brother Burdock, will strangle Brother Bean unless we see to it that he has the right of way. We can raise your great family, Brother Witch Grass, without half trying, for you have ten million children, but we prefer Brother Timothy and Brother Redtop, and we will see to it that they flourish in our acres and their moral kinsfolk in the gardens of our souls.

CHAPTER V

FARMING AS A MORAL EQUIVALENT FOR WAR

That always interesting, pragmatic philosopher, William James, once suggested that something should be discovered as a moral equivalent for war. It should be an occupation that would develop manly qualities, that would require grit and vigor, and would whet what President Roosevelt used to call the "fighting edge" of character, which at the same time would be useful for the community and state, and not destructive and barbarous as is war between men and nations. Professor James suggested various useful but humdrum employments like washing windows, washing dishes, mending roads, fishing on the Grand Banks, and the like, for the gilded and idle youth who now speed in automobiles or loll on piazzas and lead frivolous or vicious lives—a menace to society and the nation.

I think, with all due deference to the memory of the great philosopher, I can improve on his suggestions, and propose an employment which, in the classic language of the

[38]

colleges, will "put it all over" these other occupations as a useful retainer of the fighting instinct, a hardener of the muscle, a quickener of the brain, a developer of resourcefulness, and a sharpener of the will on the hard grindstone of opposition. This occupation is as old as Adam, as respectable as Cincinnatus, as beautiful as the Garden of Eden. It is none other than the ancient and honorable profession of farming.

But what I am chiefly concerned about in this article is not its age nor its respectability, but its useful development of the combative elements in our nature, which were evidently implanted for some good purpose; in fact, as my title indicates, I desire to consider farming as a moral equivalent for war. Some people are very much afraid that when all our swords are beaten into ploughshares, and all our spears into pruninghooks, humanity will deteriorate and the race of heroes will die out. Do not be afraid of this, my friends, while farms remain to cultivate, and weeds grow, and worms wriggle, and moths fly. Let no one deceive himself on this point. The Creator has furnished for anyone who owns or cultivates a rod of land, all the opposition that a healthy man needs to keep his fighting edge keen and bright.

Here is my little farm, for instance. It furnishes as good an illustration as any other. The winter's snow and rain and frost no sooner relax their hold on my few acres than the fight begins, and if I fail to be on my guard for a single week, yes, for a single day, the enemy takes advantage of my carelessness and my forces are routed.

With eagerness I waited for the soil to get sufficiently warm and mellow to sow the first seeds, and, with hope of a glorious harvest, I planted my earliest vegetables, which are warranted to withstand a little frosty nip. My peas and radishes and cauliflower were buried in their appropriate beds and lovingly left to Nature's kindly care. A little later my corn and beans and cucumbers and melons and squashes were planted, and then my tomatoes and eggplants were set out. I fancied that only my family and myself and a few kindly neighbors, who, I was conceited enough to suppose, rather envied my agricultural skill, knew what I was doing. But I was mistaken. Ten thousand little beady eyes watched my maneuvers, ten thousand wriggling creatures congratulated themselves on their coming victory.

I heard the crows in the neighboring pine trees cawing and caucusing together, and, in my manlike folly, which pooh-poohs at anything it does not understand, I said: "Those foolish crows have just one raucous note. Why can't they say something sensible and melodious?" In reality they were saying to each other, "He's planted his corn; he's planted his corn. I know where *I'll* get my breakfast tomorrow morn." Sure enough, they did, and as they got up an hour or two before I thought of rising, they were in my cornfield long before I was, and the first round of the battle was theirs. To be sure, I could replant my corn, but that was a confession of defeat, as though a general allowed his troops to be mowed down and then had to fill up his regiment with raw recruits which in turn were just as likely to be slaughtered.

The cutworm brigade of the enemy was more patient than the crows, as it needed to be. They bided their time, and just when the cauliflower and brussels sprouts and cucumbers timidly pushed their green heads above the brown soil, they captured them, gorged their loathsome bodies with the tenderest juices of the young plants, and left me defeated, with my garden strewn with the wilted and dying remnants of the crops that only yesterday gave so fair a promise. All

[41]

this in a single night. Each plant had its own worm, just one single worm, but there were enough worms to go around. It was as if the worms met together in a council of war and the general-in-chief marshaled his troops with consummate skill, assigning to each soldier his post—cauliflower, cabbage, or cucumber, as the case might be. They all obeyed orders implicitly, and I was routed—horse, foot, and dragoons.

I could have borne the disappointment and attributed it all to the notoriously uncertain hazards of war, if the enemy had been less wanton, if the worms had eaten the rations they captured; but no, they simply cut the plants in two near the ground, and left the beans to wither in the sun and the roots to dry up. They were like a regiment of looters who could eat but little, and carry away nothing, and who, for the mere fiendish pleasure of destruction, burned and ravaged everything that came in their way. However, I replanted and reset my melon and cucumber vines and cabbage plants, protected them with fences of tarred paper, placed mines of "bug earth" and "Kno-worm" around them on every side, and girded up my loins with patience once more.

By that time the battalions of the air were

descending on my trees, and I hastened to turn my attention to them. Here I seemed more helpless than before. It was as though the perfected war aeroplane had been put to this base use and the enemy came flying from the blue to discomfit me. The gypsy moth, the brown-tail moth, and, above all, the codling moth, all attacked me from above. The latter flies only by night and does not begin his depredations until honest folk have gone to bed. Then he gets in his deadly work, and, it is estimated, ruins half the apple crop of the United States by his nocturnal attacks. How cunningly he plans his campaign against this king of fruits! No Napoleon ever better understood the act of harassing the enemy. He waits until the right moment, and when he sees the blossom falling his army comes flying to the orchard. He glues his eggs to the embryo apple or near it. In about a week these eggs hatch and the little worms wriggle their way into the cup-like blossom end of the apple. Here they hide and feed for several days—then they bore their way into the very core, and the days of that apple are numbered. The apple indeed may live and grow, but it will always be a poor, knurly, wormy, worthless thing.

But the codling moth is only one of the

[43]

enemies of my trees. There are the regiments of lice that get into the leaf and curl it up; and the light infantry of the apple maggot, a tiny worm that burrows into the fruit in all directions; and the tent caterpillar that camps on my trees, and houses a thousand troops under the dome of a single tent; and the scale of different kinds, San José and oyster-shell and scurvy, all of which attack the bark. Every tree in my orchard has its own particular enemy. The cherry has the "May beetle," the "rose-bug," and the "brown rot." The pear has the "pear tree slug" and the "pear blight"; the plum has the deadly curculio and the "plum gorger"; and the peach the "peach rosette."

But not only does every tree have its own enemies; every part of the tree has its foes. The bark has its borer and its scale, the leaf its lice and curlers, the blossom its moths, the fruit its borers. Each enemy knows exactly the weakest part of the citadel he has to attack. He knows the exact moment when his attack will be most effective. He has the accumulated experience of a thousand ancestors behind him. He never makes a mistake in his maneuvers, or fails to avail himself of the psychological moment.

What, then, can I, a mere man, do with a

thousand watchful, unmerciful foes to combat, a mere man with only one pair of hands and one poor brain to oppose these multifarious enemies, or, if I do not forget to count my Portuguese assistant farmer, two pairs of hands and two poor brains at the most and best? Shall I give up the fight and call myself beaten by the worm and the moth and the crow and the weed, which I have hitherto forgotten to mention, but which is always ready to spring up and take my plants by the throat? By no means! Here comes in the joy of the struggle. Here is the delight of a fair fight and no favor. Quarter is neither asked nor given. I will oppose the wisdom and skill and resources of my kind against worm and weed and moth and bird. Come one, come all. I defy you to do your worst. I have got my artillery ready. My battery consists of two sprayers, one for the trees and one for the plants. My ammunition is of various kinds, but largely consists of Bordeaux mixture, Paris green, arsenate of lead, whale-oil soap, and tobacco tea. I spray and spray and spray again. As often as the enemy attacks, I sally out to meet him with my long and deadly tube of poison.

I do not always wait for him to assume

[45]

the defensive, but as soon as he shows his head I train my artillery upon him. It is a fight to the finish. There can be no drawn battle in this war. There can be no peace without victory. One or the other must win. Little by little I find my enemy giving way. The spraying pump drives the worms out of their fastnesses. The potato bugs give up the fight, conquered by Paris green and the sprayer. The cutworms are overcome by constant watchfulness and frequent replanting. The scale I attack with kerosene emulsion and whale-oil soap. The curculio I knock off and destroy. The tent caterpillars I burn in their own gauzy tabernacles, and lo! when the autumn comes, in spite of innumerable foes—foes that creep and crawl and fly and bore—I am the victor. My apples are rosy and fleckless; my peaches are delicious; my cauliflowers lift up their great white heads out of their chalices, asking to be plucked; my tomatoes hang red and luscious on their vines; my potatoes are smooth and spotless; my corn is full-eared, sweet, and juicy, and if I am not a better and stronger man for my tussle with nature and the enemies of my farm, then there is no virtue in war, and no value in the "fighting edge."

[46]

CHAPTER VI

UNDER THE WILLOW IN THE SPRING

I have a favorite sanctuary, where I go when I wish to be alone, and where I write my books and articles and editorials. It is under a great willow tree on my little farm at Sagamore. This is, I think, the largest willow I ever saw, or rather it is a collection of willows, for thirteen large trunks springing from one root unite at the bottom and spread out their great arms in every direction, their lateral reach being more than one hundred feet north and south. A willow likes to soak its feet in the water, and a small pond three hundred feet long and half as broad washes its roots. Around the pond are alders and viburnums and oaks and firs and a quince bush or two, as well as a tangle of grapevines, and any number of beautiful ferns. Behind rises a little hill covered with hard pines, on the top of which is "Pine-Tree Knoll."

But this article has to do not with my trees and my little pond, much as I love them, but

[47]

with the tame wild visitors that come to see me while I am writing. I have to sit very still for a while before they are quite sure that I do not want to hurt them. They do not mind my writing if my pen does not scratch, for they are all going about their own business and are perfectly willing I should go about mine.

Yesterday a red squirrel came to get a drink in the pond. He jumped from a large pine tree to an oak, and was just going down a natural grapevine ladder when a catbird spied him and determined that he should go thirsty for one morning at least. Nimble as he was, she was spryer still, for she had wings that more than matched his twinkling feet. When he ran along a limb, she flitted to the other end and screamed at him, as much as to say, "You come an inch farther, and I'll pick your eyes out!" Then he dropped to the limb below, and she flew to the one just above him and repeated her warning. Then he essayed to go down his grapevine ladder, but she was there before him to dispute his passage. At last he got discouraged, and slunk back thirsty into the woods, whereupon the mother catbird gave a triumphant scream, and went back to her nest-building in the alders. My sympathies were altogether with the mother bird, for the red squirrel is a great thief, having a special fondness for birds' eggs. Indeed, he and his kith and kin and the quarrelsome English sparrow are perhaps the worst enemies that our native birds have to endure.

I once met Ernest Harold Baynes, that great bird-lover and ornithologist, near his Bird Sanctuary in Meriden, New Hampshire. For a peaceable bird-lover he looked very warlike just then, with a double-barreled shotgun and a belt full of cartridges. But he was fighting for liberty and permanent peace in the bird world, against which the ruthless red squirrels were waging war. I should like to have heard what the red squirrels had to say about it. I have no doubt they could have made out a pretty good case for themselves.

The pair of catbirds celebrated their victory with a splendid chorus of song, for it may not be known to all my readers that in addition to his caterwauling, which is sometimes very disagreeable, the catbird has a great variety of notes and songs, and deserves the name of "the northern mocking bird," quite as much as that of the *genus felis* for which he is usually called. Moreover, he is a trim and dapper bird, with every

[49]

feather of his blue-black coat in perfect order. This trim neatness, by the way, is characteristic of all my tame wild friends. They plume and prink like a young lady going to a party, and they take frequent baths. That is one reason why my pond is so popular. It offers them both cleanliness and drink. Indeed, I think all wild creatures are careful of their toilet, and are far more fond of being specklessly clean and neat than their average human neighbor.

My next visitors today were two kingbirds, and they showed me a new trick in kingbird tactics. I have often seen them sit on a limb of a tree or on a telegraph wire, their keen little eyes alert to the flutter of every winged insect, darting like a shot from their perch and never missing their victim. But these kingbirds were fishermen as well as fly-catchers; for, seeing some water-bugs swimming contentedly on the surface of the pond, they dove for them from their perch on the willow tree, like gulls going for hapless minnows. Sometimes they would be almost, if not quite, submerged; but they never missed their prey.

The kingbird is even more of a fighter than the catbird, and is bound to be cock of the walk wherever he lives. One thing I like

[50]

about him, however; he doesn't pick on little native birds, nor even take a bird of his size, when he wants to fight, but never hesitates to tackle a bird ten times as big as himself. Even crows have no terror for him, but he constantly plagues the life out of them, as he would say, if he spoke colloquially.

But the tiny birds of my sanctuary please me quite as much as the more obtrusive ones: the warblers and the ever-cheerful chicka-dees, which will almost roost on your finger so confiding are they—almost but not quite, as a rule, except in wintertime, when a handful of hemp seed will tempt them to any degree of familiarity. I have been struck with the delicate tints of my friends, the black and white warblers or creepers, as they are some-times called. So delicate are they that you must sit very still and let them come quite near before you fully appreciate them. An opera-glass will greatly help you really to know the warblers. Then you will see most dainty colorings of red and yellow and blue as they go flitting among the leaves of a tree, looking for bugs and larvæ—thus, by caring for your fruit trees, rewarding you a hun-dredfold for any kindness you may show them, and never sending in a bill. The warblers will often repay you, too, not only

[51]

by eating noxious insects, but by sitting on a limb close to your head and rendering a solo for your special benefit, thus shaming other professional singers who will never sing except before a large audience.

I should also state that my little pond attracts larger game than squirrels and birds. At certain seasons a small herd of deer comes down to drink, in spite of the fact that my farm is within a mile and a half of a large manufacturing village. But you must be up betimes to see them; for, like other wild things, they are daylight-savers, and have set their alarm-clock at the crack of dawn. When they have had a drink, they sometimes wander into my garden, and I have noticed that they regard my string beans as a specially toothsome delicacy. However, I am willing to share with them, if they will leave a few for home use, as they usually do.

In my pond, too, are some big goldfish, which were only fingerlings when I put them in three years ago. They rejoice in the sunlight, and on a bright day in spring they come up into the shallow water and lie close to the surface, even sticking their back fins above the water, evidently enjoying the sunlight no less than I do myself. Perhaps they delight to show their brilliant sides, for Solomon in all his glory never had a coat like theirs. The horned pouts—I am glad the ugly things have so ugly a name—keep to the bottom, in the mud. I don't wonder they refuse to show off. The frogs and the turtles, on the other hand, live on the land in summer, except for an occasional dive beneath the wave, when a possibly unfriendly footstep comes too near. The turtles are very careful to sit on the edge of the bank or on a projecting piece of wood, so that it is as easy for them to take a bath as falling off a log.

One verse from the Bible that often comes to mind as I sit in my sanctuary while I write and watch my tame wild friends is, "O Lord, how manifold are thy works! In wisdom hast thou made them all: the earth is full of thy riches."

CHAPTER VII

MY DOORSTEP VISITORS

I have other friends besides those that visit me in the bird sanctuary under the big willow by the little pond. I do not have to seek them out. They come to me. I think they regard me as a special providence, for I came to my farm early this year before the snowstorms were over, and when there was little for them to eat in the woods. In fact, I was never so popular with my feathered friends before, especially after a certain April blizzard, when the snow in drifts was piled up four feet deep around the farmhouse. Then I cleared a piece of ground a few yards square, and sprinkled it with crumbs and chicken-feed, and hung up a wire basket containing a big piece of suet. You should have seen how my tame wild friends came to the feast. I couldn't entirely acquit them of selfishness; for most of them never favored me with many visits before, and I have no doubt the cynical definition of gratitude would apply to them: "Gratitude is a lively expectation of benefits yet to be received." However, though I realized that many of them were bread-and-butter friends, who would flit as soon as worms and insects became plenty, I welcomed them one and all, for friends are worth having even if their motives are not unmixed.

The sparrows were by far the most numerous of my doorstep friends, and what a variety there was! Song sparrows, the sweetest of all our tuneful birds, with their modest plumage and the three little black spots on the breasts of the gentlemen; the chipping sparrows with their reddish heads and their Quaker gray waistcoats; the white-throated sparrows with a clerical-looking necktie under their chins; and, most trim and saucy of all, the white-crowned sparrows, with their handsome heads in which a broad white stripe predominates. They are most dapper birds, and it seemed to me showed a little contempt for their more sober relatives. However, they were on a week-end visit and stayed only one day; for they were migrants, and were on their way to their nesting grounds in Canada. But they made up in numbers for their short stay, for I counted twenty near my doorstep at one time. My best breakfasts would not make them linger, and after twenty-four hours they packed up their belongings and winged their way north-

[55]

ward. The white-throated sparrows re-
mained longer, but they mostly left in the
course of a fortnight, while the juncos, which
are allied to the sparrows, stayed longer
still; and a few, I think, will be with us all
summer. The song sparrows and the chipping sparrows, like the poor, are always with
us, and never disdain friendship's offering.
Neither do the English sparrows, but *they*
steal what they get. It is never a free-will
offering that I give to them. Most people
do not realize that there are no fewer than
thirty-three different kinds of sparrows listed
in the popular bird books as found in
America, and I have no doubt several other
kinds were among my dooryard friends besides the five I have mentioned, but I am not
expert enough in ornithology to know them
all when I see them.

Still another bird that honored us with
frequent visits in the famine season of the
spring was the cowbird, a beautiful creature
when you get near enough to admire him.
His brown head has a peculiarly warm tint,
contrasting with his glossy green-black body
that glows like burnished steel in the sun-
shine. He, too, became very friendly and
very numerous, and did not disdain to pick
up his crumbs amid a whole flock of sparrows

of various kinds. But if bird-men (not avia-tors, but ornithologists) are to be believed, he or she is a sad slacker, never making her own nest, or hatching her own young, but laying in any other bird's nest that comes handy, a bluebird's, or tree-swallow's or robin's, while she lets the other birds hatch and bring up her children—a most reprehen-sible mother! When the chewinks came back from the South they also took an early breakfast or an afternoon tea with us fre-quently, though they were not so friendly as the sparrows, juncos, and cowbirds.

The robins seldom mingled with their smaller brethren in the scramble for seeds, but turned their attention largely to worms, which became amazingly plentiful when the warm rains descended, the whole yard being perforated with their holes like a sieve. It was very amusing to see the robins cock their heads on one side as though listening for a worm at his hole, then suddenly dive for it, and never miss pulling out an unwilling wrig-gler. I wonder what sort of noise angle-worms make, and whether they have a lan-guage of their own. If so, our dull ears are not finely enough attuned to hear it.

The bluebirds came with the robins, or possibly a day or two before them, and there

is nothing more lovely than to see them darting from tree to tree, as though a speck of
summer sky had been let loose and floated
down to earth.

The tree swallows came very early, too,
and, though they did not patronize our doorstep table, they did the next best thing and
circled around it, swooping down and almost
touching our heads at times as they chased
the moths and flies and other winged prey.
The gentlemen of this family are very beautiful birds, with backs and heads a brilliant
greenish blue, and white breasts; and they
have all the grace and swiftness of movement
that belong to the swallow family. In spite
of what the books say, their wives look to
me very much like them.

It is true, however, that nature in the bird
kingdom often lavishes most of her beauty
on the males, thus reversing the laws of the
human family. The lady oriole, for instance,
is a very unobtrusive little bird that you
would not think belonged in the same family
as her shining bridegroom. So is Mrs. Scarlet Tanager, whose husband is the most gorgeous of all our northern birds. The same
is true of the cardinal, the cowbird, the rose-
breasted grosbeak, and a multitude of other
lady birds.

[58]

A little later in the season than the spar-rows and warblers come our most brilliant birds, the Baltimore orioles, the scarlet tana-gers, and the goldfinches. We who live in the north are likely to think that the most gorgeous birds belong to the tropics, and do not visit our cold northern shores. It is true that the great parrot families are deni-zens of the tropics, and they are largely re-sponsible for this impression; but I have wan-dered through the tropic jungles of Brazil and Africa, and, except for the parrots, I have never seen birds that for brilliance and delicacy of coloring surpass some of our northern friends, and as for the screeching, harsh-voiced parrots, I wouldn't give an oriole, a bluebird, or a tanager for the whole lot of them. The oriole always reminds me of a piece of sunrise sky, flitting from tree to tree, while the tanager is a flame of fire, in-tense enough to set the green leaves ablaze. The goldfinch is as brilliant as any Hartz Mountain canary and as tame, and one is tempted to think that the door of a neighbor's bird cage has sprung open, and let the pets escape. The goldfinch, too, is a sociable lit-tle fellow, and does not disdain my doorstep table.

I haven't time to introduce my readers

[59]

to all the feathered friends that have called on me this spring and summer. The list would be a long one, and I have persuaded some of them to stay not only to their meals, but to lodge with me and rear their families on my farm. Not only robins and sparrows of various kinds, but bluebirds, tree swallows, flickers, and downy woodpeckers thus honored me last year; and I hope more guests will engage the houses, rent free, that I have put up for them this year. Some, however, like the sparrows, robins, brown thrushes, orioles, warblers and whippoorwills, prefer to be their own architects; and to that I will not object, since they pleasure me with their presence and their songs.

It is surprising how soon birds know where they are welcome and wanted. The little village of Meriden, N. H., has become famous throughout the country as a "Bird Sanctuary," not only because of the large tract of land set apart for feathered bipeds, but because in almost every yard they find a home. Food boxes and nests, and the universal kindness of the people, have made them so tame that they fly to their hosts, sit on their heads and fingers, and eat out of their mouths; and even in winter the snowy lawns are dotted with scores of birds that defy the

[60]

cold. Yet Meriden is no better situated than any other small town in the United States or Canada to attract the birds. The winters are cold and long, but the men and women behind the bird boxes and the food trays have made the place famous. Mr. Ernest Harold Baynes has his house here, and seems to have inspired all his neighbors with his hospitable spirit toward our songsters. The village has a bird library, and even enjoys a "Bird Sunday," when the village ministers preach on God's care for the birds, and our duty to them. Last year one hundred and one pairs of birds of no less than fifty-three different species are known to have raised families—some of them several families—in the tract of land called the "Meriden Bird Club Sanctuary," besides a multitude more that nested in other parts of the town.

There are now nearly two hundred "Meriden Bird Clubs" throughout the country, and they are found in almost every state. Why should there not be a bird club in every town for the protection of our trees and crops, and especially for the cultivation of the finer graces which love and care for our feathered friends are sure to bring to any community?

CHAPTER VIII

BIRDS IN THE BUSH AND BIRDS IN THE BOOK

Next to the joy of following our native birds to their native heath, seeing them flit from limb to limb, and hearing their joyous carols, is that of greeting them in the pages of some sympathetic author, who expresses our feelings concerning the songsters whom we love, but are inarticulate to praise. Miss Abby P. Churchill, of the State Normal School in Fitchburg, Mass., has brought together many of the best things that the poets have said about these feathered friends, in a little book called "Birds in Literature," from which I think she will allow me to cull for my readers some choice extracts.

The beauty of the writings of a genuine bird lover, who also has the literary gift, is that he can express the characteristics of the bird, apparently his very thoughts; and, as we read these descriptions of the various common songsters of our woods and fields, we realize the distinct individuality of each bird and the particular place which Nature has assigned him in the great orchestra of the woods. For instance, what could be more characteristic or exactly descriptive of the bluebird's well known habit of flitting from fence-post to fence-post, as one walks along the country roadside, than Lowell's lines:

"The bluebird, shifting his light load of
    song
  From post to post along the cheerless
    fence."

The bobolink, next to the robin, perhaps, has inspired the song of more poets than any other bird. Of him C. P. Cranch says:

"When Nature had made all her birds,
  With no more cares to think on,
She gave a rippling laugh, and out
  There flew a Bobolinkon."

Bryant, who always had an ear for birds as well as for all melodies, has written a well-known poem of considerable length about "Robert of Lincoln," the first stanza of which is as follows:

"Merrily swinging on brier and weed,
  Near to the nest of his little dame,
Over the mountain side or mead,
  Robert of Lincoln is telling his name:

[63]

Bob-o'-link, bob-o'-link,
Spink, spank, spink;
Snug and safe is that nest of ours,
Hidden among the summer flowers,
Chee, chee, chee."

Naturally the robin occupies much space in the poet's calendar, though he is by no means, in my estimation, the most charming of our American birds; for he is often quarrelsome, and at certain times of the year he has a monotonous chirp which is almost distressing. However, he forces himself upon public notice. He has no undue modesty. He is a good advertiser, and so he stands more distinctly than any other bird for the coming of the springtime. Scores of poets have eulogized not only the robin redbreast as we know him, but the truer robin redbreast of Great Britain, whose name and memory our homesick ancestors transferred to the common thrush of our own woods.

Here is what Lucy Larcom says of Sir Robin:

"Robin, Sir Robin, gay, red-vested knight.
Now you have come to us, summer's in sight.
You never dream of the wonders you bring,
Visions that follow the flash of your wing;

[64]

How all the beautiful by and by
Around you and after you seems to fly!
Sing on, or eat on, as pleases your mind!
Well have you earned every morsel you
  find.
'Ay, ha! ha! ha!' whistles Robin. 'My dear,
Let us all take our own choice of good
  cheer.' "

The robin has the great advantage as a self-advertiser of coming very early in the spring; sometimes, in fact, he stays with us throughout the whole winter. He is often preceded, however, by the bluebird and one or two inconspicuous warblers. Thus his early appearance, before the woods are vocal with the songs of a thousand of his mates of different size and plumage, makes an impression not only upon us people of prose, but upon the poets, and once caused E. C. Stedman to sing:

"The sweetest sound the whole year 'round:
  'Tis the first robin of the spring!
The song of the full orchard choir
  Is not so fine a thing!"

But many of our "common or garden" birds have attracted the attention of poets, as well as the few favored ones. I imagine that few of my readers know how charming

[65]

a singer the catbird is. As I have said, he
is well called the "northern mocking bird,"
for he has more songs in his repertoire and
more notes in his vocabulary than any other
of our northern birds. Minot J. Savage has
well characterized the varied parts that he
plays in the bird orchestra in a rather
long poem, which ends as follows:

"Catbird, but I love thee still,
By the brookside, 'neath the hill,
Laughing, mocking in the trees,
Feathered Mephistopheles;
Playing out thy varied part,
Mirroring the human heart;
Fretting, scolding, scornful, then
Bursting out in joy again.
    Good and evil catbird
      On the alder spray,
    Like thy contradictions
      Run our lives away."

Even the crow has his biographer, if not
his eulogist, among the poets, and Clinton
Scollard has asked this question of him, and
received this answer, which we oft hear him
give as he sits on the topmost branch of a
dead pine tree:

"O, say, Jim Crow,
Why is it you always go

With a gloomy coat of black
The year long on your back?
Why don't you change its hue
At least for a day or two,
To red or green or blue?
And why do you always wear
Such a sober, sombre air,
As glum as the face of Care?
I wait for your reply.
   And into the peaceful pause
There comes a curious, croaking cry,
   'O, because! 'cause! 'cause!'"

I wish I had space in this chapter to introduce you to all my feathered favorites, or at least to tell you what the poets can say of them so much better than I can say it; but I cannot close without writing of my greatest favorite of all, the song sparrow, the modest, little, brown-coated, unobtrusive bird, which comes so early in the spring, and stays with us so long, and never, as many birds do, forgets his song the whole summer through. He is trim and neat, but has no distinguishing features which mark him as a brilliant beauty; and yet of all the birds there is not one which seems to have more genuine thoughts of praise in his heart, or offers them with such tuneful and joyous abandon. I see him at almost any hour of the day on a little bush near my house, pouring out his whole soul in melody.

Florence A. Merriam tells us that "the student who is interested in noting bird songs will find the song sparrow's well worth study, for it varies remarkably. Fifteen varieties of its song have been noted in one week, and the same individual often has a number of tunes in his repertoire." Thoreau calls him a poet who sings all summer, and says: "Any man can write verses in the love season. . . . We are most interested in those birds that sing for the love of music and not of their mates, who meditate their strains, and amuse themselves with singing, the birds whose strains are of deeper sentiment." And here is what Henry van Dyke says of him, and he exactly expresses my feelings and love for the dearest little warbler of all:

"I like the tune, I like the words:
  They seem so true, so far from art,
  So friendly and so full of heart,
That if but one of all the birds
  Could be my comrade everywhere,
  My little brother of the air,
This is the one I'd choose, my dear,
Because he'd bless me, every year,
With 'Sweet-sweet-sweet-very-merry-
  cheer.'"

CHAPTER IX

OUT OF DOORS IN THE AUTUMN

Here I find myself once more writing under the old willow, as in the springtime six months ago. Then the catkins were just beginning to show the white feather, and I had to look closely to see that the oak buds had begun to realize that spring would ever come. Since then they have swelled and burst, and the oak trees have tossed them on their branches for many a long day, defying old Boreas, who lives on Cape Cod all the year around. Today some of these oak trees are one great, glorious pyramid of flame, redder than any maple that incarnadines New Hampshire's granite hills. Other oaks clothe themselves in modest browns. I notice that, though the leaves of the flame-colored oak have begun to fall, but very few are yet upon the ground; for an oak makes up for its late appearance in the spring by clinging to its foliage late in the autumn. Indeed, in some varieties the brown leaves rustle on the cold twigs all winter long, until the young buds actually push them off, saying, "Get off my perch; it's my turn to have a look at the world."

The leaves on the big willow are all gone; the precious catkins look dry and dead; and the clinging grapevines that festoon the lower branches of the willow seem sick, discouraged, and frostbitten, while the oaks flaunt in their faces their gayest colors. So it is often with precocious children. They use up all their bright sayings while they are young, while the steady plodder who develops late lasts long. Whether this generalization is true or not, it is a comfort to us mediocre fellows who never had any bright sayings recorded of us in our childhood.

My English friends sometimes gently deride me for various Americanisms which they are pleased to note, and one of them is the use of the word "fall" instead of "autumn" to indicate the ninth, tenth, and eleventh months of the year. But after all it is a most expressive term. As everything is springing to new life in the third, fourth, and fifth months of the year, and we call that season "spring," so everything is falling in the later months. How the leaves swirl down as they fall in the fall! The rosy apples demonstrate over again Sir Isaac Newton's great discovery; the woodchucks dig themselves in, and fall asleep; and the turtles on my little pond follow suit. Yes, it is the falling time of the year, and there is nothing sad about it if we only remember the great law of nature, that everything must fall to rise again. The leaf must fall, or we can have no buds next year. The apple must fall if we are ever to have another crop. We must fall asleep before we can wake. We must die before we can share in the resurrection. I am not sure which is the more delightful season, the spring or the fall. Spring is the season of hope and anticipation. Fall is the time of fulfillment, of peace and plenty. The pile of big, yellow pumpkins about the farmhouse door, the smaller mound of white carrots and red mangel-wurtzels, the barrels of apples and potatoes, all add their joy to the fall— joys which the spring can only anticipate.

But to get back to my seat under the old willow. The birds are still with us as they were in the spring, but they seem more subdued and quite tongue-tied. I hardly hear a chirp, though the fly-catchers are still darting after their winged prey, and the creepers are searching for other inhabitants under every rough piece of bark, and the woodpeckers are using their bill-hammers industriously. But in the spring how the birds did chatter as well as sing! I imagine they were consulting about housekeeping and the care of the children, and those are always prolific subjects of small talk. Then Mrs. Catbird insisted on building her nest in the jungle of bushes near the pond, while Mr. Catbird was afraid that it would be too convenient for the snake or the red squirrel. But the lady had her way, I think, as she usually does. The birds were courting, too, in the spring; and that involves an immense amount of chatter and no end of love songs. Now they are sober old married folks, and though very likely they are still fonder of each other, they find fewer things that must be said.

Yet there are some exceptions to the rule of taciturnity. The blue jays are just as noisy and impertinently talkative as ever. What saucy, bright, immaculately dressed creatures they are—every feather always in place, their crest always brushed up *a la pompadour*, not a speck of dust on their sleek blue coats. But, beautiful as they are, they are always scolding about some real or imaginary wrong. They remind me of a beautifully dressed but saucy maiden, with a sharp tongue and a high-pitched, unmelodious voice. One can love a bluebird, modest yet friendly, with a sweet tongue which she does

[72]

not use too much, but who can love a blue jay?

Neither have the crows lost their voices. Three or four of them have just come over to my willow as I write, "winnowing their slow way through the air." I think the little flock consists of a father and a mother and two children, for the voices of the young ones are as different from their parents' as a young rooster just beginning to crow is different from old Father Chanticleer. They all landed in the willow before they saw me sitting beneath it. Then how they did scold, father, mother, John, and Mary! "Caw, caw, caw! Go away, away, away. This is my tree. What are you doing here?" But I held my ground despite their scolding, and soon they flew to another tree several rods away; and—would you believe it?—when they had settled down to a family conclave, their voices changed to a quiet, conversational tone, almost a cooing note. I had never listened to crows talking together before, or heard any but their jarring, rough, raucous voices. My respect for the whole tribe rose after hearing this little family conversation, even though I knew they had just been stealing my ripe corn.

The red squirrel that in the spring I had

[73]

seen coming down the grapevine ladder for a drink in the pond came again today. He, too, like the crows, resented my presence, and chattered something like, "Get out of here; get out of here." But even he was not so vocal as in the spring, when he had his fight with the catbird. I did not move in spite of his protests, and he soon departed for my cornfield which the crows had left.

There is still another creature that has not lost her voice in these autumn days, and that is the chickadee. Dear little symphony in black and white, how cheerful and optimistic you always are! In the coldest winter weather you never forget your one little song or your friendly good nature. You will perch even on a snow-covered twig, just beyond the reach of my hand, and never seem to get cold feet. Anyway, if you do, they never make you grouchy. I must very soon fill my suet cage for you. I am going to remember you at Thanksgiving time as one cause for gratitude. You are well worth it.

But before Thanksgiving Day most of the chickadees' feathered companions will have sailed southward on their individual aeroplanes. They are already gathering together in large flocks, for, like the war fliers, they prefer to go in squadrons. To be sure, the chickadees will stay all winter, and the blue jays and the crows, and an occasional robin and flicker; but most of my winged friends will not much longer haunt the willow pond. Some will go to South Carolina and Florida; others, without passports or baggage, will cross the international boundary to Mexico and Costa Rica, while others will fly still farther and settle on the slopes of the Andes. It is a far cry from Cape Cod to Capricornus, but you will make it safely, I doubt not. God be with you till we meet again; and, when you come back in the spring I hope to be here to meet you. How I wish you could tell us of your wonderful journeys and the strange things you have seen and the people you have met! Yours would indeed be a traveler's tale worth hearing.

CHAPTER X

A RAINY DAY AT THE FARM

It is very fortunate that all days are not "brite and fare," or else we should miss the peculiar joys of the rainy day at the farm.

We draw up the blinds in the morning for the first glimpse of out of doors. Good, it gives promise of a long, rainy day. The clouds are of that unbroken, somber gray that allows no peephole for the sun. It is not yet raining, but the weatherwise will wet his finger, and thrust it out to see from what quarter the wind blows. Good, again; it is from the northeast, for both Boreas and Pluvius have a liking for that quarter. And, listen! can you not hear a faint rumble from the direction of the sea? It is not pronounced enough yet to be called a roar, the breaking waves are not yet dashing high, but the wind is beginning to raise the whitecaps, and soon the long slow boom of the sea will add its music to the soughing of the pine trees. There is no hurry about taking it all in at once. It will not be a rainy hour but a rainy day, perhaps two or three days,

[76]

and one can enjoy it slowly without fear of missing anything.

The first duty, if we must have duties on rainy days, is to see if there are dry logs enough beside the big fireplace to last forty-eight hours, without stinting ourselves of a single cheerful tongue of flame. Not quite enough, and so, before the rain comes down heavily, we will stagger in under half a dozen logs, one at a time, each one of which is all we want to handle. The old fireplace has a capacious and insatiable maw. Have I mentioned that its mouth is seven feet wide at the front and four feet wide at the back—its gullet, so to speak? It could take in half a cord of wood at a time if we wished to be extravagant. And indeed we need not be sparing, for we are rich in scrub pines and oaks, and old, decrepit apple trees. ·The former need to be thinned out, and the latter to be chopped down, and John hasn't much else to do in midwinter, so he provides a good store. Moreover, we are depriving no one else of fuel in these shivering days of high prices, since transportation from the old farm would cost more than the wood is worth. So we can pile on the logs with a good conscience, only being careful not to put on so many as to roast us out of house

[77]

and home, and drive us away from the ruddy blaze.

Of course there are other fireplaces in the farmhouse, four of them, to say nothing of a fifth which vandal hands once bricked up, but they are only little three-foot affairs that take stovewood. They are well enough for an hour on a chilly morning, but are not to be thought of for a long, rainy day.

There are not coals enough in the ashes of last night's fire to start a blaze, so we will use the "Cape Cod Fire Lighter." This, as is well known, is a piece of porous stone on a stiff wire handle, kept when not in use in a bright brass pot half full of kerosene oil. The stone holds the oil for ten minutes after it is lighted, a sufficient time to set fire to the toughest old logs, if a few soft wood sticks are at the bottom. The more orthodox way of lighting the fire would be to whittle up some shavings, lay them deftly under the big sticks with enough open spaces to supply them with oxygen, then rake a coal out of the ashes and let nature do the rest. But we have to make some concessions to modern life, even in the old farmhouse—hence the Cape Cod Fire Lighter.

Now the rain begins to come down in earnest, not like a summer shower in big, driving drops from a black thunder-cloud, but steadily, from a leaden sky, as though it meant business and intended to keep at it all day. As the drops chase each other down the window panes the blaze, which has now seized firm hold of the big logs, goes in the other direction, and mounts higher and higher in the big chimney. It roars and crackles and leaps up as though glad to be free of earthly shackles. Perhaps it is the spirit of the wood, which has been bark-bound for fifty years, drenched with sap, and held down by fibrous tendons for two or three generations, and is mighty glad to get into the free air once more.

It may be something like this with our own spirits, one of these days, when at last they are free from the bonds of "earth and sense." I can easily imagine it of the martyrs who have gone up from the stake in a chariot of fire—John Huss, Jerome of Prague, Latimer, and Tyndale, and perhaps many a poor Negro, horribly lynched for a crime he never committed. What is that hymn we used to sing to a swinging tune?

"Rivers to the ocean run,
    Nor stay in all their course;
Fire ascending seeks the sun
    Both speed them to their source.

[79]

So my soul, derived from God,
  Pants to view His glorious face,
Upward tends to His abode,
  To rest in His embrace."

How easy it is on a rainy day before a big fire to drop into poetry, like Mr. Wegg—not original, of course, but acquired in childhood.

We are not afraid of a roaring blaze in the old fireplace. The house is insured, that's one comfort, and it is doubly insured by the heavy rain on the roof, which would kill any sparks as soon as they touch it. At any rate we remember with satisfaction that the house has stood for two hundred and thirty years and has never yet burned down; that, undoubtedly, thousands of cords of wood have gone up in that old chimney in smoke and flame; and that, in all probability, there have been far more reckless firebuilders than we in the seven generations that have warmed themselves at that hearth. We trust the old chimney.

How many methods of producing light and heat have come and gone since the first blaze lighted up that chimney, before George Washington or Ben Franklin was born! First the flint and steel and tinder, or perhaps the friction of the pointed stick, twisted

[80]

Indian fashion, which the Boy Scouts are so proud of making today. Then the live coal, carefully covered up in the ashes or borrowed from the nearest neighbor if our own farmhouse coals had lost their glow during the night. Many a frosty morning, I warrant, little John or Jane ran over to Neighbor Crowell or to Neighbor Swift to "borrow some fire." Not a few people now living remember when that was a common practice. Then came the old, smelly lucifer match— the very name as well as the smell suggesting the lower regions—and the tallow candle made by hand by dipping. Then the whale-oil lamp without a chimney, smoky and dull; then the first rude kerosene lamp, then gas, then the electric light, and the Cape Cod Fire Lighter.

Gas and electricity the old farmhouse has never known. It would seem almost a desecration to introduce them. But fire and light were the same glorious boons before any of these new contraptions for making them were invented, and the ruddy blaze warmed the knotty knuckles of the first farmer who built my house, and lit up the rosy faces of the little towheads who gathered around the fireplace, quite as well as in these sophisticated days.

[81]

The fire is so interesting that I had almost forgotten the rain, but that is as charming in its own way; at least the sense of contrast between the howling storm outside—for it has begun to howl—and the peace and warmth within has all the elements of quiet joy. I go to the door, but do not care to stick my head out too far—just far enough to get a splash of rain in my face, to teach me what I do not need to face.

I listen to the boom of the breakers on the shore, half a mile away—for they have begun to boom in good earnest now—and I offer a silent prayer "for those in peril on the sea" and think of the many times I have paced a steamer's deck in just such a gale, or heard the waves dash against my stateroom port with an awful smash, as though they would surely break through, while the big ship shook and shivered with the shock. But storm warnings have been up all along the coast for twenty-four hours, the papers have predicted this storm, and few if any mariners in frail ships will be caught in it. So I can enjoy the storm, without too many compassionate thoughts to dull my pleasure.

From the east window I can see the white rollers dashing over the breakwater of the Cape Cod Canal, as it juts out into the big bay. It is like a great gleam of flashing light on the angry coast that comes and goes with every wave.

There is not much life outdoors on the farm today. Irene, the Jersey cow, and Imogene, the Angora goat, are in their snug houses, for though they can stand a gentle rain and rather like it, they have no stomach for a northeaster. Onesima, the big pig (the Bible will tell you why a good lady gave her this name), with her little litter, is under shelter and so are the hens, for they have no relish for wet feathers, not being well oiled like their neighbors the ducks who revel in such weather. Beauty and Jack, the two St. Bernard dogs, came to the kitchen door for their morning dog biscuit, but they soon turned tail and sought their kennels, while Tabitha, the cat, never would put her dainty paw out of doors on such a day as this and much prefers the braided rug in front of the fire.

Later in the morning Portuguese John in oilskins and sou'-wester comes with the *Boston Herald*—but who wants to read of Presidents and cabinets and leagues and treaties and New York and New Haven stocks on such a day? Let it stay in its wrapper for once.

[83]

I will go into the library—it was the best parlor in the original days, with beautiful hand-carving around the windows and mantelpiece—and choose a book. What shall I choose? My modest literary riches embarrass me. Shall it be "The Tempest," writ by a certain W. Shakespeare, who didn't know how to spell, and could scarcely write his name legibly? I think not. The tempest is out of doors, and I will read it from the window.

One book isn't enough for such a day. I will take two or three. One shall be a copy of Bushnell's sermons, a superb book, for I feel in a serious though happy mood, and a good sermon isn't such dry, tough reading as most people suppose. I will take, too, "The Anatomy of Melancholy," one of the least melancholy of books, for it, too, well fits into the mood of the day, and also one of Archibald Marshall's tranquil but absorbing novels. It will be either "The Greatest of These," or "The Honor of the Clintons." I won't touch "Sir Harry," for I am tired of war books and war stories. Dear authors, give us a rest from blood and carnage!

I shall not read all of these books, perhaps not any of them, but I like to have them by me. So I will take them all out, and

[84]

wheel the big green plush chair—which some little children call "Grandpa's ch‑i‑"—in front of the fire, and pile the books up on the rug at my feet. Yet I presume that I shall read the book in the flames most of the time, as they leap and flare and die down, and the white ashes decorate the charred sticks with delicate lace, until I pile on more wood. As Lizzie Hexam in "Our Mutual Friend" used to read to her brother Charlie the fire stories in the "hollow down by the flare," so I can read my own books there, more beautiful than any printed page. Why bother with Bushnell or Burton or Marshall today, good as they all are?

I wish all my children and grandchildren were here to enjoy the rainy day with me. It would be a noisier, merrier day, but business and school keep them all away at this time of the year. Only one other is in the old house, and she has been with me for many a pleasant and many a rainy day, for four and forty years. People will persist in calling us "elderly," though it is hard to tell why, when we feel almost as youthful as we did four times ten years ago, and four more added.

No outsider comes in to cook the simple meals. We draw a little table up in front of the fire, wheel the one-course dinner (no table d'hote) in from the kitchen on the tea wagon, toast our bread before the glowing coals, and, with plenty of Irene's clotted cream and yellowest butter, have all that heart can wish. In memory of the former days, and to remind the old fireplace of what so often happened there a hundred years ago and more, we pop some corn over the coals and roast some apples on the hearth, and then play a game of Colorito—a complicated but interesting game with counters for two. We will also have some reading aloud, which we both greatly enjoy.

All this is after the blackness of a fall evening has shut out the rain and tossing trees and breakers, and has shut us in to quiet peace and to each other. As we go up to bed in the great square room overhead (no stived-up seven-by-nine bedroom for our ancestors!) the rain is still pattering upon the roof and dashing against the windows—the sweetest of all lullabys.

In my school days the more or less mushy boys and girls used to write in each other's albums such sentiments as this:

"Into each life some rain must fall,
Some days must be dark and dreary."

[86]

I am glad some rainy days have been my lot. They have been far from "sad and dreary." Indeed, at the close of such a day I can say, "Thank God for the rain and 'stormy wind fulfilling his word.'" Indeed, I have come to "the end of a perfect day."

CHAPTER XI

THE UNDERGROUND ALCHEMIST

Another cold, hard winter has come and gone, and here I am, sitting once more under the big willow beside the little pond in the "sunken orchard." Not that the orchard itself ever sank; but my predecessors, a hundred years ago or so, took advantage of one of the innumerable hollows of Cape Cod, scooped out by the glaciers in prehistoric times, and planted here some Baldwins and Porters and Russets and one or two delicious summer apple trees whose names I do not know. The trees are very aged and gnarled, and some of them are decrepit; but, like the righteous man, they "still bring forth fruit in old age," even if they are not fat and flourishing.

As I write, the leaves on these old veterans are about the size of a mouse's ears, which shows me that it is time to plant corn. By the way, I see that a controversy on this question is raging in the daily paper I take. One correspondent says the time to plant corn is when the maple leaves are as big as a mouse's ears. Another says that is too soon, and that we must wait till the ash leaves are of that peculiar size. Still another writes that both are wrong, and that oak leaves, the latest of all, must measure up with a mouse's external auditory organ before it is safe to plant corn. I shall, perhaps, rashly differ from them all, and stick to my old apple trees to tell me when to plant the sweet maize which all good Americans love. As I sit here, the young willow leaves afford just shade enough, but not too much, while the warm May sun, flickering through the mouse-ears of the apple trees, dapples the sides of the sunken orchard; and I am "lost in wonder and amaze" at the strange things that are going on underground in this spring-time.

Talk about alchemy and the transmutation of metals! The old alchemists couldn't hold a candle to this unseen alchemist of spring-time, even if they had been able to change all the baser metals of the world into gold and silver. Think of it! Something is taking place out of sight in the brown earth beneath the grass that will transmute the elements in the soil and air and rain into ten thousand different products. The roots of the apple trees will suck up certain juices and minerals and transform them into leaves and blossoms, and, after awhile, into fruit. I see a white pine growing beside the apple trees, and that will get something else from the same soil and air and rain. It will never grow an apple, but resinous pine needles, sweet and fragrant. On this side of the little pond is the big willow under which I am sitting, and to which I have before introduced my readers. It will always find willow food, but never any apple juice or resin, though its roots must almost intertwine themselves with the pine's and the apple's not fifty feet away.

Festooned from branches of the willow is a big grapevine, planted no one knows when; for it bears a delicious fruit unlike any modern grapes that the nurserymen sell. Its roots are now feeling about in the spring soil, saying to Mother Earth: "I want some grape substance. Don't give me willow food or pine-tree stuff, but that juicy, flavorsome combination which you have furnished me every spring for the last fifty years, so that I can hang my purple clusters on the willow branch next September." Mother Nature hears the grapevine's plea, and furnishes the ingredients for which it asks.

Ten feet away on the edge of the pond are

a dozen black alder bushes, and they want something different still; for they expect to bear no apples or grapes or resinous cones, and they do not wish to reach out their arms like the willow in every direction. They wish only to grow about ten feet high and to bear clusters of white blossoms and no end of berries, which the robins and catbirds will be so glad to get just before they fly away in the autumn.

But here is a still more wonderful thing that the underground alchemist is at work on during these spring days. He is planning to give a different flavor to each of my varieties of apples and a different color to their skins. How vast a number of pigments and essences he must have in his secret cupboards! Over there is a big Porter apple tree. Its oblong, rather daintily shaped fruits must have a yellow skin and a spicy and rather tart flavor. A Baldwin tree stands next to the Porter, Dame Nature, and you must see to it that its apples are rounder than the Porter, with a deep-red blush on both cheeks, and a sweeter taste, which I cannot describe exactly, except that it is a Baldwin-apple taste. There, only two rods farther off, is a Golden Russet. Be careful, O Underground Alchemist, not to get your flavors or colors mixed; for I expect my Russets to have the lovely, velvety brown skin, and the exact, old-fashioned Russety taste, when I come to eat them next April; for a Russet isn't really good until six months after it has been picked.

There is another point which the alchemist never forgets, and that is to put a different time limit to each kind of apple; for we can't have them ready to eat all at once, lest some of them spoil. The Summer Harvests, which I forgot to mention, must have still a different color and flavor scheme from all the others, must be ready to eat in August; and Porters must be in their prime in September. Baldwins may be eatable in November, but will be better still in January; and as for Russets, I will barrel them up and not touch them until March at the earliest. So it would be a great mistake if things got mixed in our underground laboratory, and if I should find my Summer Harvests hard as rocks in August and my Russets half rotten in September.

I am wondering, as I sit here under the willow, whether each man or woman was not meant by the Creator to have a flavor and color of his or her own. Some of us, I believe, were meant to be unusually spicy and some unusually sweet. Alas! Some of us are sour and some are knurly; but I do not think Providence designed that. Somehow we have extracted the wrong juices from life's experiences, and have turned what was meant to be a pleasant flavor, free from insipidity, into an acrid tartness. Just here we differ from the apple tree, and can pick and choose, at least to a limited extent, what our flavor shall be. I have known some people who sweetened and mellowed as they grew older, and others that soured and became more and more crab-apple like. Still, to a very considerable extent our native juices make us what we are, and it is the part of wisdom to develop along Nature's, that is God's, lines. If you are a red Baldwin, young friend, don't try to become a yellow Porter, but seek to be a flavorsome Baldwin of the very best kind. Many a good, honest Russet has spoiled himself in trying to become a Lady's Finger or a Northern Spy.

Neither let us become impatient with God and ourselves if we mature slowly. Some people are brilliant in their early days, the admired of all admirers, sprightly, popular, precocious; and sometimes these same people, like a very early apple, are rotten almost before they are ripe. Then there are others who do not reach their best estate, like my

Russets, until the frosts of winter whiten their hair. This thought is a real comfort for us slow developing folk. If we abide our time, we may yet justify the Giver of every good and perfect gift, even if these gifts are exasperatingly slow in developing.

But a truce to further moralizing. If each of us has a flavor and a color of his own, and a time of full maturity, as I believe we have, let us take courage, thank God, and make the most of these inherited gifts, remembering that our roots stretch out to another world, and reach into eternity; and "it doth not yet appear what we shall be."

CHAPTER XII

FUN ON THE OLD FARM

I think we shall agree substantially that fun is not all of the boisterous, rollicking kind that ends in a guffaw, but may also be of the gentler sort that brings a smile to the lips and a glow to the heart. I do not by any means despise the former; but the fun on my small farm is for the most part of the latter kind, and is of a sort in which birds and beasts, things animate and inanimate, may join.

As I step out of the old farmhouse door, I can almost detect a grimace in the contorted, twisted limbs of the ancient apple trees that have been blown upon by the seven winds of heaven for a century; for I have spared some of them just because they are so gaunt and gnarled, though I have little hope of future fair Baldwins or Greenings. Even in their winter bareness they seem to be laughing at the wild winds, as much as to say: "We are too much for you, old Boreas. You can't uproot us if you do your worst. You may twist us and blow us out of shape; but,

[95]

old as we are, we can defy you still, as we did when we were young, a hundred years ago." It is not in the winter, however, but in the spring that Nature is in her jolliest mood. Then every new spear of grass and unfolding bud says: "Why, here I am, as fresh and sweet as ever. The ice didn't freeze my veins, and the snow was a warm coverlet, and I have had such a good, long sleep that I have waked up in the happiest possible frame of mind, and am good for at least six months of joyous life."

It will be seen from this that I am not a gentleman farmer, with a great estate over which I ride once in a while, and leave all the real work to my underlings. I cannot think there would be great fun in this. No, I like to take hold with my swarthy helper and plant and spray and trim and prune. To be sure, he does more than his share of the rough work, and much of the year I must be cultivating other kinds of fields than those that grow cabbages and turnips; but the fun of farming comes from being a real farmer while you are one, getting close to the soil, becoming intimate with every living thing, whether it be a plant or an animal, loving your tomato-vines and raspberry-bushes, taking a real pride in your eggplants and in

[96]

your Brussels sprouts, whether you get a prize for them at the county fair or not.

Then there is the fun of trying new experiments. I never lose my faith in the annual seed catalogue in spite of divers and sundry disappointments. With new zest every year, as I have already said, I read of those wonderful strawberries, one of which would fill a tumbler, and the ever-bearing raspberries that are in fruit from June to December, and the mammoth squashes which only a Hercules can lift. I am very sure to try some of them and get any amount of fun out of my anticipations of similar results. No matter if the realization falls far short of the picture in the gorgeous catalogue. I lay the results to my poorer soil, or lack of skill in cultivation, and have just as much confidence in the novelties which next year's spring catalogue exploits as the "very largest, richest, juiciest, most melting (always a favorite word) fruit in the world." I would not lose my faith in the seed and fruit catalogues for all the squashes and raspberries that grow.

But there are some unusual things which one can always do on a farm, which relieve the monotony, if one finds any, in beans, corn, potatoes, and cabbages; and variety is not

[97]

only the spice of life, but the soul of fun on the farm. You can, for instance, raise peanuts anywhere in the east—not large crops, to be sure, but a little experimental patch; and yet not one person in a hundred north of Mason and Dixon's line ever saw the delicate peanut vine and its pretty yellow blossoms. The same can be said of the sweet potato, whose foliage is lovely, and of the okra, with its beautiful flowers that would reward you for your pains if you did not care for chicken and gumbo soup. There are a dozen other vegetables and a score of flowers which, though common enough elsewhere, are seldom raised in your vicinity, and watching whose development will afford interest and pleasure the whole summer long.

Then there are freaks in the ordinary vegetable and flower world that add not a little to the fun of farming. For instance, last summer I saw that one specimen of kohl-rabi on my farm gave evidence of outdoing all his brethren in size. So I did not pluck him in his green and succulent state, but bade him do his best. He grew all summer long until he became a very Daniel Lambert among his fellows. His sides bulged like a balloon; his very eyes stood out with fatness, as the Scriptures say of the wicked man; and I could imagine the other vegetables pointing the finger of derision at him, and calling him "Old Fatty," and "Tubby," and like opprobrious names. The Chinese must have a sense of humor, I think, since they prefer to have their ginseng roots, by which they set so much store as a medicine, in the form of a man, with two legs, two arms, and a round bullet head, as it sometimes grows. Such roots, I understand, bring five times as much in the market as ordinary ginseng tubers. What other extreme value can they have except an appeal to the Oriental sense of humor?

When it comes to flowers, how good a time one can have on a small farm in watching the development of odd shapes and colors! Scatter a handful of portulacca seeds in the soil, and you can no more count the colors and tints which this sun-loving flower presents than you can count the shades in a glorious sunset sky. Bury some dahlia bulbs in the spring, and by midsummer you will have a score of shades, single and double, fringed and plain, small and big, and a hundred different colors as well.

Oh, there is always something new on the small farm. Its infinite variety largely adds to my pleasure. It is never stale nor

[99]

monotonous. It never repeats itself. Every morning in summer I go out with eager anticipation to see what new development the new day has brought, what new green shoot has pierced the brown soil, what new bud has opened, what new fruit has begun to ripen, what new flavor my melon vines have yielded, what new odor comes from the flower bed. The Psalmist's words are as true of all living things as they are of the heavens:

"Day unto day uttereth speech,
And night unto night showeth knowledge.
There is no speech nor language;
Their voice is not heard.
Their line is gone out through all the earth,
And their words to the end of the world."

And then the animal life on my small farm! It is as much fun as a menagerie. Every morning the big woodpecker wakes me up at sunrise, or a little before. "Tap, tap, tap," he calls on the old shingles, searching for the insects that are hiding beneath. "Tap, tap, tap, you lazy fellow," he says. "The sun is up; why are not you? I have been awake since dawn, getting grubs for my little ones. Get up, get up, get up." I obey his summons, and watch him fly down from the roof and disappear in the round hole that he has drilled in a rotten old apple tree which I have left standing for his benefit. Of Giotto, the famous builder of the beautiful cathedral and campanile in Florence, it was said that his work was as perfect as the round "o" in Giotto. The same can be said of the work of my friends, Mr. and Mrs. Yellowhammer, or Mr. and Mrs. Highhole, or Mr. and Mrs. Flicker, by whichever name you care to call them. The hole they have made is as round as the "o" in Giotto. It could not be a more exact circle. I cannot quite put my hand in, but I know the cavity is full of their offspring; for when I tap on the bark and put my ear close to the hole I hear a hissing sound, as tense and sibilant as though a whole crowd of gallery gods was trying to drive an actor off the stage.

After a while a great, fat, goggle-eyed youngster will come to the hole, filling it up completely, and, like an "end-seat hog" in the street-car, preventing any of the others of the brood from crowding by or coming to the front. But he dares not leave his natal hole in the apple tree yet. His wings are weak and untried. In a few days, however, when I go to visit him again, he is not there. Suddenly he mustered up courage to try his unused powers; and a quick dart from the big apple tree, a gleam of mottled yellow, a flicker through the light and shade of the orchard, and he is gone. I hope he will come again next year to hammer on the roof of the old farmhouse, to wake me up as his father and mother did this year.

As for my domestic animals, they are of all degrees of humor. Of course, my collie puppy is just a bundle of fun and good nature and awkward gambols. He seems fuddled with animal spirits. As for my cow, I can't see that she has any sense of humor at all. If I stroke her nose, or rub her back, or give her a choice cabbage leaf, she takes it all as a matter of course, as though it was her due. She has no smile of recognition and no "Thank you, sir," for me. My pig grunts his thanks as plainly as can be, and there is a twinkle in his eye that says, "My gratitude is exactly proportioned to the number of ears of corn you gave me."

The two geese, Hero and Leander, that live in the little pond—Leander swam the Hellespont, you know, "for to see his dear" —are too much engrossed with their own self-importance to have any time ever to look on the kindly, humorous side of life. Like some men I know, they go through life without once suspecting how ridiculous they are, so wrapped up are they in their own self-conceit. They waddle around side by side, never suspecting, apparently, that they have not the most graceful gait in the world. This I will say for them, however; they are a most devoted pair. No husband and wife were ever more true to each other. "I will never desert Mr. Micawber," Hero seems to be constantly saying, while as for Leander, he is certainly always waiting for something to turn up in the way of a grasshopper or a feed of corn. My ducks are much more lively and humorous than the geese. Nothing pleases them so much as to pick a choice morsel right out from under the noses of Hero and Leander, and then waddle off at twice the speed the geese can make, and splash into the water, with a "Quack, quack, quack," which I can interpret as meaning, "You didn't catch me that time, old slow-coach, did you?"

As for the hens, they are unconscious humorists. They are always funny, but they never know it. George Fitch once said that a hen will run twenty-five yards for the sake of crossing a road in front of an automobile, when she never wished to go across until she saw the auto coming. My hens often run off with a piece of string or paper that happens to be in their feed, apparently for the

[103]

sake of fooling the other hens and making them run violently after the possessor of the string. I have sometimes thought that this shows a tendency toward practical joking; but, on the whole, I am inclined to think that a hen isn't bright enough for that, and that this is only another illustration of the fact that she is funny without meaning to be.

Who would ever go to a movie or a vaudeville show when he could have so much higher class fun on a small farm?

CHAPTER XIII

ALWAYS SOMETHING NEW ON THE OLD FARM

The charm of the old farm is perennial. It always has something new to offer. There is scarcely a day of the three hundred and sixty-five and a quarter, that I do not find something to look at that I never saw before. To be sure, a few rough and icy days in winter may seem to furnish an exception to this rule, but even then wonderful new patterns of ferns and arabesque tracery of all sorts are drawn on the window panes. I like to go down cellar, even on the coldest days, to see if the winter weather has not added a new flavor to my Baldwins and a new mellowness to my Russets. If these material good things should fail of novelty, the farmhouse library has untold treasures, so old that they are new to most people of this generation.

But with the first breath of spring come the new things that I have chiefly in mind. There is the rhubarb patch, tart reminder that even the sourest experience of life can be so sweetened as to become delicious and refreshing. A bulbous sign of coming stalks breaks ground even in March, when there is scarcely another green thing to welcome it. The next day a tinge of red shows itself; the day after, the big bud unfolds and, almost before I know it, a great leaf as big as an elephant's ear is inviting me to pick, stew, and abundantly sugar the juicy stem that upholds it.

The asparagus bed lies next to the rhubarb, and is its close rival for an early resurrection. One morning I scan the old bed. Surely that is the spot where I plucked the luscious stalks last year. But it gives no sign of life. "I must wait another week," I say to myself. However, as I stroll by the next day, there is my first Palmetto, with its head neatly overlaid with scales like a soldier's helmet to enable it the better to push its way through the hard soil. And there is another, and another, and another. If I were a woman I believe I would take my knitting and sit down and see the asparagus grow, for tomorrow morning those shoots will be six inches high and twice as big around as they are today. Being a man, and having nothing to occupy my hands, I can only wait until tomorrow morning comes to pluck the "grass" for dinner.

Then follows a quick succession of novelties, morning after morning. Indeed, I have to go over my farm twice a day to keep up with them. As the buds begin to swell, the plum trees and the cherries are running a race. One day I think one of the rivals is ahead, and then the other. At last the plum trees win out, but only by a lap. At least they do in Japan, and I think it is true also of most American plums. First a few adventurous buds unfold, and then suddenly one morning I draw up the shade of my east window to see if it is likely to be a "pretty day," as they say in the south, and lo! my plum trees are all huge bouquets. If it were a little earlier, I would think they were covered with snow. The pear trees lag a little behind the plums, but not much. In fact, the Duchess and Bartlett are out before the petals fall from the Abundance and the Burbanks. They stand up straight and perky on their stiff twigs, as though they would say to the sprawling, lopsided Japanese plums, "I'm not much behind you, and at any rate I am much more trim and symmetrical."

Then the apple trees, as though spurred on by their more forward brethren, begin to blush at being such laggards, and almost before we know it they are all ablaze with bloom, and make up for any dilatoriness by offering the most magnificent spectacle that the whole orchard affords. I envy the man who never saw a great apple tree in blossom and who has that sensation in store. Suppose he had seen nothing but tropical vegetation all his life, and some day, having just landed in the night from some equatorial port, should open his eyes the next morning on a New England or an Oregon apple orchard in May—every tree one great mass of pink and white! What would he say? Unless pride of country and climate kept him quiet, I think he would say, "This is the rarest flower in the world, and I would give all my orange blossoms and my gorgeous bougain-villias and poinsettias for this one apple or-chard." And yet we berate the barrenness and sterility of our northern climes, and long for the glories of the colorful south!

The beauties of the trees, however, shall not blind my eyes to the small new things that, following the apple blossoms, peep shyly from the brown earth. Those potatoes that I planted in April were most unprom-ising looking slabs of inert material. But they seem to know that they must help feed the nations and make the world safe for Democracy; and one morning, a fortnight

[108]

after, I find row after row of little new leaves forcing their way up into the sunlight. Few things are more wonderful than the way Nature, the oldest of alchemists, transmutes an inert, lifeless mass of starch and protein into a delicate, tender plant, which the potato bugs, at least, think is most succulent. We wonder at the butterfly coming from the chrysalis which the dying worm spins for his winding sheet, but that is not a bit more remarkable than the transmutation of half a decrepit old potato into a bushy plant, with a whole family of delicious young tubers clustering about its roots.

Indeed, there is something delightfully and surprisingly new about every young thing, whether it is a plant or a baby. The beans pushing their twin cotyledons above the soil, the corn urging his spear into the sunlight, the melon peering timidly above the soil as though afraid of a frost or a cutworm —each has its own special charm and each gives me something new to watch for, every bright spring morning.

And not only does inanimate nature furnish my farm with novelties—I take the word back, I will not reproach my potatoes and beans with being inanimate. They are not without *animus*. How sadly that word

[109]

has degenerated in our English use! At least, the One who makes them grow is not mindless, and He seems to have put something of His *animus* into them. I am not sure that they are not sentient. But, for the sake of conforming to popular prejudice, I will make a distinction between the corn and beans and the chickens and little pigs. At least they have this in common, that both at the beginning are very new and charming. "When will the old hen come off?" is a question that the children ask half a dozen times a day. I am almost as eager as they are to find out. And sure enough, one morning there are twelve little fluffy new things peeping out from under Mrs. Brown's feathers, every one as fresh as the first brood that came up with their clucking mother, asking Adam for a name. The new calf makes a great sensation on my old farm, and so do the eight little white pigs, and the grandchildren can scarcely go to sleep at night lest they should miss something wonderfully new.

Spring does not bring all the new things, by any means. Indeed, the year never grows old, though we often speak of it in an uncomplimentary fashion, as the "old year" or the "dying year." There are quite as many new things in July and even in October as in

April or May. The first strawberry, at least on my farm, does not usually come until June, though this last year I did get a box from my ever-bearing vines on the 31st of May, which filled me with bucolic, but I hope not sinful, pride. The first raspberry comes late in June, and the first good blackberry in July. It is just as new and quite as delicious as though it came in April.

My land! (if ever this old-fashioned expletive is in order, it is now) what a lot of new things come along in July and August! The first Red June plum belies its name, at least where I live, and is not fit to eat until July. Then, too, a little later the Abundance plums almost break the boughs, each one as deliciously new as though there were no other. Then comes the first Mayflower peach, followed by the J. H. Hale, whose name, though he himself recently died, lives in a thousand orchards. I know of no surer way to achieve early immortality than by giving your name to a really good peach or grape or apple. It will last longer than sculptured marble, and when Old Mortality must needs go around to dig the moss out of the letters of your name on the tombstone, a delicious fruit will carry it down untarnished to the third and fourth and, for all

I know, to the thirty-fourth generation. Who was the first Mr. Baldwin, and the first Ben Davis, and the first Mr. McIntosh, and the first Mr. Porter? I suppose some horticulturist knows, but a million of us common people, without knowing who they were, call over these names every summer or autumn. This brings me back to my subject, and to remember that my first Porter apple I will pick in August, but my first Baldwin I will let hang on the tree until October, though he will scarcely be worth eating until December. The same is true of my first McIntosh Red, but then his flavor will be as fresh and delicious as though he were a Summer Harvest and ripened in July.

If we look for them, we shall find almost as many new flowers in September and October as in May and June. Then the asters and the goldenrod are in their glory and if in May I ruthlessly pick off the blossoms from my ever-bearers, I can have fresh strawberries in November. I often wonder, how Dame Nature can hold back her children so as to give us births almost every month in the year. I should think that asters and goldenrod and altheas would feel the urge of springtime and hasten their blooming, instead of waiting until many of their companions are in the sere and yellow leaf. One would think they would hear the lilacs and the shadbush and the cherry trees in April and May crying out, "Come on and come out, you lazy things. Don't you know it is spring, and time to bloom?" But they bide their time, and know that they will be all the more welcome when the riot of spring and early summer are past. My Baby Ramblers, too, and my Soupert roses and my geraniums will bloom until a nipping frost seizes them, giving new buds and blossoms every day until near December. As for the late Crawfords and Greenboros, they are not good to pick until the "nipping and eager air" of autumn comes, and my Brussels sprouts and parsnips like to be frozen a little before they yield me their best.

So the season rolls around on the old farm, and brings a new joy with every day of every month. Farming monotonous? I should say not. Business is the same old routine, summer and winter; school-teaching palls upon the most enthusiastic teacher before the summer vacation comes; preaching is sometimes undeniably dull work in hot weather; but the farm is perennial in its joys, unfailing in its novelties. Who would not enjoy the daily crop of new delights on an old farm?

[113]

CHAPTER XIV

NEXT BEST TO A FARM

I am sorry for a man who cannot own a farm, however circumscribed or sterile its acres. Yet I know that some unfortunate sons of Adam are so beset behind and before by business cares that a real farm seems out of the question. There is but one thing for such a man to do and that is to become a suburbanite.

I know that it is a vast come-down from the wide horizon of even a small farm to a ten-rod garden, and it seems small potatoes to measure your land by feet and not by acres. But when "needs must" holds the reins, we must go at his pace. The suburbanite is deeply conscious that there are thorns on his rosebush and it is not to be supposed that he can escape the ills that afflict our common humanity. He is more or less tied to trains or electric cars or automobiles, but, then, trains and cars and autos are growing more and more numerous and extending farther into the suburbs and thus continually lengthening his tether. His friends are said to know him by the bundles which his capacious arms bring out of the city every night. But if he is the happy possessor of a long, green bag, he can stow away in it anything from a turkey to a half-pound of peppermints for the children or a bunch of catnip for Tabby, and no one through its opaque sides can get a glimpse of the details of his domestic economics or economy. Other friends declare that the suburbanite is known by the anxious and haggard look on his face, caused by a perpetual anxiety to catch the 8:23 train, and by the different colored threads on his fingers which his wife has tied there "lest he forget" the prunes or the baking powder or the castor oil for the baby.

But these calumnies may be all set down to the envy of the urbanites, or, if there is a sediment of truth in them, think how much time the suburbanite has, both morning and evening, to smooth off the wrinkles in the glorious hours of sunrise and sunset and to untie and throw away the good wife's remembrance threads! But to speak with all seriousness and out of personal experience, I may say that next to a farm, I would choose a suburban home for three reasons: for my family's sake, for my body's sake, and for my soul's sake.

First, for the family: Think of bringing

[115]

up a family of children in the city, when you might rear them in the country or at least the semi-country! Think of the boys' having no coasting or skating or canoeing or swimming without going miles to get them! Think of the girls' being obliged to take a train to find an hepatica in the springtime, or having to take a trolley ride even to see a dandelion! Think of a dogless, henless home, and perhaps even a catless home! To be sure, one can own a cat or even a dog in the city, but it is a poor circumscribed, joyless existence that old Tray must live there, and only a spoiled and petted lap-dog can be happy when continually in sight of brick walls and sidewalks.

But though cats and dogs are not impossible in the city, guinea pigs and rabbits and ducks and hens, to say nothing of turkeys and peacocks, are quite out of the question. There is no such humanizer of boy nature as pets. The lad who has a tame squirrel that will eat out of his hand, a dog that will tumble all over himself and split his throat with glad barks when his young master proposes a walk, or a colt that will come whinnying at his call, will never grow up to be a cruel bully.

And hens! What a vast education a boy can find in a flock of these feathered bipeds!

[116]

They teach him mathematics, economics, hygienics, and the rudiments of I do not know how many other sciences. "How much will seventeen eggs at sixty-five cents a dozen come to?" If Father does pay the bill, the young hen fancier must reckon up his profits every week, and find out at the end of the month the difference between the cost of a bushel of shorts and ten quarts of second-grade wheat, on the debit side, and five and one-third dozen eggs on the credit side. Then there is the study of the fascinating hen magazine, and the delightful possibilities of "200 eggs a year per hen," and the arguments for and against dry feeding and a hot mash, cut alfalfa, grits, and charcoal—all of which are an education in themselves. If a duck pond can be added to the suburban estate, however small it is, the fascination is almost doubled. But even in the tiniest there is room for a couple of rabbits and a few bantams.

The snow fort in the winter, the flower garden in the spring, the swimming pool in the summer, the chestnut trees in the autumn—only the suburban boy or the country boy can know what they mean, with all their manifold and exhaustless charms.

But I have said that if I could not have a

farm I would choose a suburban home for my own sake as well as for my family. The hardest thing for a professional man to do is to keep in such good physical condition that he won't be a nuisance to himself and his friends. Dyspepsia is another name often for peevishness, and nervousness is a synonym for all-round misery. Surely a man who can breathe fresh country air at least fourteen hours out of the twenty-four, who can work in a garden and walk in the fields, has a better chance to discipline his stomach and his nerves than his all-the-year-'round city neighbor. Better than all the setting-up exercises in the world, valuable as they are, or the physical culture fads which one begins upon so bravely and which usually "peter out" so soon, is the physical culture which you do not know you are getting when you are pruning your grapes, and tying up your clematis vine, and burying your tulip bulbs in the mellow brown soil of spring.

Besides this, a suburbanite usually lives within walking distance of some golf-links, and when his small garden is cared for he can shoulder his clubs and chase the elusive ball over hill and dale, until, thoroughly tired and thoroughly at peace with the world, he is called home by the dinner bell. If one has

[118]

no taste or time or money for golf, a very small suburban estate contains endless possibilities for exercise. The front lawn alone is enough to keep a man in good condition if he looks after it himself. A multi-millionaire in one of our western cities, who was often seen pushing his lawnmower over his half-acre, was asked why he did not hire a man to cut the grass. "Can I hire a man to sweat for me?" was his gruff but all-sufficient reply. To be sure, on many soils a lawn is an expensive luxury, and I sympathize with the suburbanite who declared at last, after many unsuccessful attempts at grass, that he had decided it would be cheaper to carpet his front lawn with Turkish rugs. Yet if he had reckoned the healthy perspiration which the care of the lawn had started, there would have been a large balance in favor of nature's green rug.

But I have said that considerations of soul health also would influence me in choosing a suburban rather than a city home. Soul health, after all, is the most imperative. Though a man can possibly be a saint in the city, he has a better chance of sainthood, in my opinion, in the country. Some men can see God in bricks and mortar, in artificial parks and fountains that can be turned on

[119]

and off with a stop-cock, but most men can
see Him more clearly in hill and valley and
running brook. There are sermons in stones,
but they can be read more easily before the
stones are built into walls. A noble grove
of pines is more apt to remind me of their
Maker than is a skyscraper, even if the stones
and brick clay of which it is built did come
originally from God's country. To pluck
a humble little pansy that I have seen grow
from a seed that I have planted and watered
and watched reminds me more of the Giver
of all good than does the most elaborate
decoration of a gilded palace. To see things
grow, just to see things grow, seems to make
the soul grow with them. The expanding
maple leaf in the spring, the tasseled chestnut
in the early summer, the gorgeous gladiolus
in the fall, the Mayflower bud waiting under
the leaves through the long winter, each remembering his appointed season, remind one
throughout every day of the round year that
"the hand that made them is divine." However tiny the leaf or flower, it tells the same
story.

"Flower in the crannied wall,
  I pluck you out of the crannies,
  I hold you here, root and all, in my hand,
  Little flower—but *if* I could understand

What you are, root and all, and all in all,
I should know what God and man is."

I shall only add to the suburbanite homily
a word about the quiet mornings and peaceful evenings of the country. The midday may
be full of bustle and confusion, worry, and
possibly heartache, but the morning and evening hours frame in the day with a beautiful
border that seems to make the whole day
lovely. The cares of the working hours slip
away, and the soul is bathed in peace when
the sun goes down, and when he rises again
one can begin the new day with a quiet hour
—even if the "hour" is only fifteen minutes
long—of meditation and inbreathing and
soul-expansion. This is not impossible, to be
sure, in the city, but how much more fragrant
is the hour in the country on a summer's
morning, as one whispers to himself Mrs.
Stowe's beautiful lines, before he goes to the
dust and toil of the city:

"Still, still with Thee, when purple morning
        breaketh,
    When the bird waketh, and the shadows
        flee;
Fairer than morning, lovelier than daylight,
    Dawns the sweet consciousness, I am with
        Thee."

[121]

CHAPTER XV

CAN A HORSE LAUGH?

"It's enough to make a horse laugh," said my neighbor Jenkins to me the other day, rehearsing a story that he considered excruciatingly funny. Whatever the merits of the story, it implied an undeserved reflection on the sense of humor of old Billy, who was demurely grazing nearby but just out of hearing. How does Jackson know that Billy does not understand a joke unless it be a particularly obvious and uproarious one? Bring him a peck of oats, and if he doesn't laugh when he sees you coming with them, I don't know what a horse laugh is, and anyone that can laugh must have a sense of humor, unless it is a sardonic, Mephistophelean chuckle in which I am sure honest Billy never indulges. I have already written of some of the signs of fun I find on the old farm, but the subject is so prolific it deserves another chapter.

I wish that the indefatigable gentleman who spent some weeks in a monkeys' cage learning the simian language had recorded a monkey's skit on the men and women out-

[122]

side his cage, or even an apean limerick. I am confident these Darwinian cousins of ours have their jokes. Anyone who has watched them in a big banyan tree in India, gently spanking their little ones but with a great show of force, or sidling up to another monkey on a precarious limb and then giving him a sly push that sends him off the branch, compelling him to take a flying leap, knows how fond they are of practical jokes, at least.

"Isn't he stuck on himself!" said a small boy, as we were watching the antics of some monkeys in the Zoo, one of whom was intently gazing at his face in a mirror and making all sorts of grimaces, which he evidently enjoyed. My opinion, however, was more complimentary, for I attributed his facial contortions not to personal conceit but to that very human sense of the ridiculous that makes the contorting mirrors at the circus the most popular of all the sideshows. What shrieks of laughter the fat man provokes when he sees himself and others see him as a lean and hungry Cassius, a veritable beanpole of a man. The tall, thin man equally amuses himself and all his friends when the convex glass shows that he has suddenly become rotund enough for a dime museum. So the monkey in the Zoo was enjoying himself in

[123]

the same way, only he was making the distortions for himself—another proof, it will be seen, of our cousinship.

But I set out not to write of humor in the monkeys' cage, which is evident enough, but of humor on the old farm, which is just as real if not so boisterous. There is the big sow, for instance. She is about as unpromising a subject as one could pick out. Yet a year ago, when she weighed only ten pounds, she enjoyed romping and playing with her little brothers and sisters, putting up a mock fight, and having a race with them all for her mother's "bosom," as Portuguese John euphoniously calls the porcine maternal font. Now, to be sure, with her ample girth, her five hundred pounds of ham and spareribs to carry around, and family cares involved in rearing her own thirteen little white darlings, she cannot express her enjoyment in the same frisky way, but I am mistaken if there is not something more than contentment in her face when after rolling in the mud she stretches herself at full length in the sun and invites her children to their fourth midday meal. If the captious critic asserts that enjoyment and good spirits are no proof of a sense of humor, I defy him to prove that **Mrs. Genus Sus** has no such sense. The

[124]

burden of proof lies with him, since it is certainly true that good humor and humor are at least closely allied in the Genus Homo.

It is interesting to note that all young things on the old farm seem to have the "saving sense." An old hen is apparently as humorless as she is stupid. I have already dilated on this lack in her mentality, but she is worth another line. She is so intent on getting every tidbit away from her sister hens and enjoying it all by herself, that she has no more time for fun than for the other amenities of life. Her eagerness to get there first and get the best seems to addle her brains, just as selfish miserliness dulls the wits of humans. When she sees her companions being fed, though the door to the hen-yard is wide open, she will strive frantically to break through the wires which have foiled her a hundred times in the past and will race down and back a score of laps, instead of seeking the open door which she must know perfectly well is there, if she would only stop and think. Thus greediness overreaches itself, and the profiteer who would hog all the best things finds a moral wire fence which he cannot pass between himself and his goal of happiness.

But with small chickens, as with children,

for the most part it is different. They are selfish, to be sure, but they are willing others should have their share if they can get it, and if I am not very much mistaken my two little cockerels have a genuine sense of humor when they bristle up, look daggers at each other, ruffle their feather boas for a minute, and then suddenly drop their apparent Hunnish frightfulness and go to picking at a spear of sorrel, as though they had always been the best friends in the world. I am sure this is part of their fun, and no real enmity is in their hearts. They are just playing that they are on opposite sides of the Piave. And later, when one of the cockerels mounts a pile of seaweed, which John is storing up for next season's potato crop, and utters his first challenge in a cracked and squeaky voice, he is only shouting like other boys of his age,

"I'm king of the castle,
And you're the rogue and the rascal."

He knows that it is a joke, and that he is sure to be deposed from his castle very soon.

My cow is a solemn creature as I have before opined. No glint of humor lights her meditative eye as she chews her cud, and when I approach her with a few carrots she is eager enough, but betrays no spark of genial fun or even gratitude in her eagerness. But how different when she was a bossy six years ago! She had not been on "this goodly frame, the earth," twenty-four hours before she began to kick up her awkward, untried heels for a frolic, and in a month she could haul the desperately resisting hired man all over the place when she did not want to follow his lead.

The old cat, too, is staid as an eight-day clock and, even with cream on her whiskers, tries to persuade you by her demureness that she hasn't been near the milk pan. Possibly, however, that is a sly species of humor for which I had never given her credit. But when she was a kitten her own tail was so amusing that she would chase it for half an hour at a time, and every ball of twine contained unlimited possibilities of fun. So, alas! it is with most of us. We forget as we grow older that there is a rainbow in every bubble if we would but look for it, and we take our pleasures more and more seriously.

Of all the animals on my farm my dogs retain their youthful good humor the longest. They are of the St. Bernard strain, and Beauty, though several times a prolific mother, will play with her grown-up son,

Jack, as though her years were the same as his. In their elephantine way they will knock each other over and playfully bite each other's ears, and lock their teeth into each other's jaws, yet never draw a drop of blood or provoke so much as an angry yelp.

A dog's humor depends largely upon his breed. Pure St. Bernards are too stately and serious to see the funny side of life, and my dogs get their fun from some alien strain. The genuine St. Bernard is always looking for an exhausted wayfarer and should never go out without a little keg of prohibition cordial around his neck. The Dachshund, too, is a solemn as well as an absurd little beast: "long and low like a bench," as Mark Twain said, "to be continued in our next." I never saw a Dachshund smile. Why should a Hun dog smile, anyway? The Boston Terrier is too conceited to be humorous. The tighter his tail is screwed up, and the more sinister the snarl on his undershot jaw, the more he thinks of himself. He will hardly speak to any dog off Beacon Hill.

Of all the dogs of my acquaintance the collie has the truest sense of humor. Whether it is the pawky Scotch humor of his forbears I am not certain. I do not think it is, however, for since he came to America, it is too outspoken and expressive. He is never contented to say of a meaty bone, "It might be waur." If ever a dog smiled with genuine mirth and good feeling, it was old Sandy when I used to come home from a long journey. As plain as voice and eyes and tail could say it, he would tease, "Now let us have a little romp, or go down town together."

But humor and good humor are by no means confined to the domestic animals. Even the tame wild birds on the old farm show that they often see the lighter side of life, in spite of their usual absorption in picking up a living. In the spring they are almost all eager for an amorous frolic, as they chase each other from limb to limb and through the air; and though the cares of housebuilding and family rearing curb their spirits somewhat, I have observed that they indulge in more than one innocent joke on each other.

Not that I think the cowbird's joke is innocent, when she lays one of her big eggs in the box I put up for the bluebirds, and which they had already preempted. It is a dirty, low joke at the best, but I can imagine the dusky cowbird chuckling to herself as she says, "Won't dainty Mrs. Blue

[129]

be surprised when she finds she has an ugly duckling in her family?" I enjoy much better the fun of the kingbird when he dashes off after a crow ten times his size, jumps on his ancestral foe, gives him two or three sharp pecks, and soars away before old Corvus can turn around. That is genuine and humorous retribution, for the crow deserves all that is coming to him. And yet Corvus himself is not destitute of humor when he sits on the scarecrow's rakish cap and flies down every now and then for another kernel, only to return to the observation tower which someone has kindly put up for him.

You would suspect from the very note that gives him his name that Bob White was a cheery little fellow, with a streak of fun in him, and when you try to find him in the weeds and long grass you are the more sure of it, for his "bob white" is most elusive, as though he were playing a game of hide and seek with you. When you are confident you have located him, he is sure to be somewhere else, and his cheerful "I spy" lures you on for another fruitless chase. If by any chance you run across Mrs. White and her little Bobs are near, she will droop one wing until you are sure that it is broken and you can catch her. But she will keep just out of your reach until you are far enough away from her nest, when she will scurry away on both wings which are really as sound as they ever were. I know that the solemn ornithologist will assure you that it is only mother love and fear for their young that move the quail and other birds to such deceit, but I feel quite confident that when well out of harm's way and the family is reunited, they all chuckle over it, and the mother bird says, "Didn't I fool that fellow nicely? These great gawky folks are so easily taken in."

The bluejay has a raucous kind of humor, like a scolding fishwife in whose Billingsgate, nevertheless, there is something sharp and funny. I imagine he is up in the latest bird slang, and if any of the birds talk back he can give them much better than they send.

The English sparrow is of all God's creatures so self-centered and selfish that I look for no gleam of humor in her practical, businesslike eye. "Everyone for herself and the hawk take the hindmost," is apparently her motto. Even her nest, which I took joy in robbing, shows no signs of nice adjustment, as though she said, "I'll trouble myself just as little as possible for my dratted young ones," and so she huddles together some

[131]

sticks and straws and calls it a nest, while her cousin, the chipping sparrow, nearby, lines hers beautifully with moss and horse-hair. How can one look for any of the sweet amenities of life in such a bird!

The chickadee has a pleasant, loquacious humor all his own. Especially in the winter, when other birds are scarce, he will don his best black and white clothes, and come more than halfway to meet you and cry out cheer-ily, "Chick-a-dee-dee-dee," which, being in-terpreted, means, "Here I am, you see, see, see." As you walk along the well-worn path, he keeps up with you in the small trees just about even with your head, but flying in and out, and perching just long enough as you go by to say again, "Chick-a-dee-dee-dee, chick-a-dee-dee-dee. Now you see me and now you don't, see, see, see." Dear little fellow, the snappiest cold weather and the iciest twigs do not seem to curb his spirits! Would that I could bear the cold blasts of adversity as cheerfully!

Of all my door-yard neighbors this last summer the tree swallows seemed to me the most sociable and the most delicate in their humorous view of life. I had early in the spring put up several nesting-boxes for them, which they accepted without any ifs or buts.

[132]

CAN A HORSE LAUGH?

The bluebirds looked at the boxes suspiciously, and for a long time debated whether to accept my hospitality or not. The robins and chickadees and sparrows of various kinds declined with thanks and said, "We prefer to build our own." But the tree swallows said at once, "With pleasure," and started their homes in the most conspicuous boxes they could find and those nearest the house.

During the period of incubation, in which I think father and mother both took part, they showed the greatest interest in all the members of the human family. We could scarcely go out of the front door but the bird on the nearest nest would stick his or her beautiful, glossy, green head out of the little hole in the nesting-box, and watch every movement with beady, black eyes that seemed to shine with merriment. When we had visitors, each in turn would show off with the greatest alacrity, flying off, circling around the tree half a dozen times, darting in again at the rate of fifty miles an hour, but never missing the tiny hole by a hair. Then he—I use the masculine gender as embracing the feminine—would turn around, stick out his head, and with his twinkling eyes would seem to say, "Isn't that going some?

Thank you for making my doorway so narrow that no crow or bluejay or snake or weasel can get in, while I can make it even when going at express speed." When the young ones left the shell the parents had little time for conversation, but every three minutes from purple morn to dewy eve one or the other would bring an insect to the hungry little maws, while they darted in and out like lightning, always getting their prey, like true sportsmen, upon the wing.

An acute observer could doubtless discover many more indications of humor among the beasts of the field and the fowl of the air, but even a layman without an opera glass and with a very limited use of his imagination can see enough such signs to make him feel a delightful sense of kinship with all created things. A sense of humor is one of the "bonds of perfectness." No one can hate or despise a fellow-being with whom he shares a good quip of any kind.

No wonder St. Anthony preached to the fishes at Rimini when the people would not listen to his sermons, and St. Francis, we know, preached to the birds whenever he got a chance. These blessed saints are not usually classed with Mark Twain and Artemus Ward, but they knew how to tell the

[134]

people of their day that even a fish or a bird was a better listener than they, and I consider that first-class ministerial humor.

But I hear Beauty and Jack barking at the kitchen door, and they plainly say, "Have done with all that humorous nonsense and give us our afternoon dog biscuits."

CHAPTER XVI

EVER-BEARERS AND EVER-BLOOM-ERS

I would, if properly I could, spare my readers the dictum of Dean Swift about the worth of the man who made two blades of grass to grow where but one grew before, but it gives me the opportunity to say that if there is truth in that overworked aphorism, then we should call down still larger blessings on the head of the man who induced a strawberry bed to bear for five months in the year instead of one, and a rose garden to bloom from frost to frost, instead of for one brief fortnight in a month, when scores of other plants are competing with the roses for first prize. Yet these strawberries and roses are both well established horticultural wonders of the day. I picked the first mess—most unhappy word to use in this connection, I admit—of strawberries on the last day of May, and the last one on the second day of November, and in the inter-calary months had a great many dishes of "doubtless the best berry God ever made," if we accept Izaak Walton's judgment. The

[136]

baby ramblers that line either side of the brick walk leading to the front door of the farmhouse began to bloom in June and found it very hard to leave off blooming in December.

Who would not throw up his hat for such berries and such roses? They take up no more room in my few precious acres, they require no more attention, and they are even hardier than their forbears, who gave my forbears only a few scanty days or weeks of pleasure. How did you bring this about, Mr. Plant Wizard? Is your name Burbank or just plain John Smith or George Jones? I wish I knew your name and address, for I would send you a letter of thanks or dedicate my next book to you— not that I consider that an adequate honor, but what else has a poor author to offer?

Your creations have done more for me than to provide me with unlimited strawberry cake and countless bouquets—they have caused me to look within and to confess that I am neither an ever-bloomer nor an ever-bearer. If one does not indulge in it too freely, introspection is as good for the soul as confession, whose virtues have so long been lauded. Yet I gain some comfort from the fact that the "common or garden" strawberry is well worth raising, and the old-fashioned tea rose which lives its little life and fades so soon does brighten my garden most wondrously while it lasts.

Of this also I am reminded, that even my ever-bearers are not equally prolific during all the bearing season. If I would have an abundance in September, I must pick off the blossoms of early May. It seems a cruel thing to do, and though I nerved myself to sacrifice a whole row of blossoms, I kept saying to myself, "I am not simply picking off and throwing away a lot of little inconspicuous white flowers, I am picking off future strawberries. There goes a whole saucerful of delicious ruby red berries. There goes a strawberry cake. There goes the best part of a fruit salad." However, I courageously kept on to the end of the row, and yet I could not altogether discourage those wonderful plants, for they insisted on putting forth new blossoms and bearing a goodly number of berries in June, but more in August, and still more in September. So, Mr. Plant Wizard, you cannot altogether annul the laws of nature. She will insist on taking a little rest. She will not let even one of your strawberry plants work twenty-four hours a day and thirty-one days a month.

On one of my Baby Ramblers—I shall spell my baby with capitals this time, however the proofreader may rave—I counted five hundred and thirty-eight buds and blossoms at one time, and the bush was not too large for a flower-pot on the center table, had I chosen to bring it indoors. Yet I noticed that even this brave plant, ambitious to outdo all its companions in the row, looked wan and exhausted after this, and dwindled away to a meager score of blossoms for a while before it really gathered strength for a new effort.

So it is in the human flower garden. No man is equally brilliant and intellectually prolific at all times. The most noted authors occasionally have a fallow-ground year, and those whose books have the greatest reputation sometimes disappoint their publishers and the public. Indeed, it is scarcely safe for an author to strike twelve the first time, lest the next hour struck should prove to be one. Do you remember Frank Stockton's story, "His Deceased Wife's Sister"? The author's first novel was so entrancing, so extraordinarily good, that for many years he could never equal it. The publishers all refused his subsequent stories, on the ground that they were inferior to "His Deceased

Wife's Sister." They said the public expected something equally brilliant, and that his reputation would suffer should they publish anything less good. For a time the poor author, unable to get anything published, pined and almost starved, but finally succeeded in getting some good, though second-rate, stories accepted and was again acquiring a fair measure of prosperity. Again he wrote a novel that in his opinion was quite as good as the first. In this his intimate friends agreed with him, and his publisher as well, who offered him a large price, but he would not risk its publication lest once more he should be involved in a like disaster. So one dark night he took it out into the middle of a lake, tied a big stone to the manuscript and sunk it to the bottom. So let us of mediocre worth take comfort that our fortune and happiness are never thus imperiled.

There is some warrant for the assertion that "good poets, like good people, die young" when we remember Thomas Chatterton, "the marvelous boy who perished in his pride," and by his own hand. He had written some beautiful poems and had hoaxed all the literary antiquarians of England with his pretended discovery of ancient manuscripts. Some saner poets died before they had rounded out their first quarter of a century, like Henry Kirk White, whose hymns we still sing, Richard Gall and Robert Nicholl, two Scotch poets of great promise, and chief of all John Keats, who died of consumption at twenty-five. It was said that his decline was brought on by the rough handling that his poems received at the hands of the reviewers. Byron, for one, called them "the driveling idiotism of a manikin," and when Keats died, perpetrated these cruel lines concerning his literary sensitiveness:

"'Tis strange the mind, that very fiery par-
    ticle,
Should let itself be snuffed out by an ar-
    ticle."

Alas, the late war has been responsible for the early death of several young poets whose swan songs were uttered to the accompaniment of bursting shell and booming guns.

Still, all these instances of the early demise of the gifted do not make out a strong case for the superiority of poets who die young, or by analogy for roses that will bloom and die in a week. I admit the beauty and charm of both, but I still prefer the

Tennysons and Wordsworths and Longfellows, the Holmeses and Lowells and Bryants and Whittiers, who wrote until old age palsied their hands, and I prefer my ramblers and my Souperts that blossom all summer to the most exquisite creation of my garden which today is and tomorrow is cast into the oven—or fireplace. It always seemed to me a sad waste of nature's energies to spend a hundred years in bringing a century plant to bloom and then to let the precious product die in a night.

To sum up the lesson of my ever bearers and ever bloomers—they teach me, though I said at the beginning I cannot claim to belong to either class, that if I would bear any fruit in old age, if I would be even moderately "fat and flourishing," I must conserve my resources. If I would have an abundance of strawberries in September, I must be chary of their fruit in June. If I would have even a few strawberries and a few roses on the table all summer, I must not make too large drafts on the vitality of my plants in their early days. A man may have "a short life and a merry one," but if merriment stands in his mind for dissipation, he cannot have both. So, whatever energies we dissipate in our youth, we lose for old age.

I always suspect the wisdom and lasting worth of the "boy preachers," and the early prodigies of intellectual might are often eclipsed before they reach their noonday.

Here is a happy thought with which to end my book: What does immortality mean if it does not mean bloom and fruit in the far regions beyond this little world? After all, my strawberries and roses are not the best symbols of constant blooming and bearing but my sturdy apple-trees, which for fifty years have blossomed every spring and borne fruit every autumn and have never altogether disappointed their owners. Yes, I would covet the blessing which the writer of the first Psalm bestowed upon the man whose "delight is in the law of the Lord," for he shall be "like a tree planted by the rivers of water, that bringeth forth his fruit in his season; his leaf also shall not wither; and whatsoever he doeth shall prosper."

www.ingramcontent.com/pod-product-compliance
Lightning Source LLC
Chambersburg PA
CBHW020949030426
42339CB00004B/13